A year of
BEAUTIFUL
WOMEN

Geoff Howe

View the sensuous side of photography
through the lens of a top professional

PSL

Patrick Stephens Limited

ACKNOWLEDGEMENTS

Grateful thanks to all those who helped me in the preparation of this book, including my good friend Simon Redfern, who collaborated with me on the writing when I finally managed to concentrate his mind; both our families, who patiently put up with our agonizings; Graham Walkling, who put in many late nights designing it; Alison Roelich and Darryl Reach of Patrick Stephens Ltd, who still kept faith with us despite our rather elastic view of deadlines; Ralph Medland, for being there; and all the models and clients who made the pictures possible in the first place.

© Geoff Howes 1992

First published in 1992

British Library Cataloguing in Publication Data: A catalogue record for this book is available from the British Library.

ISBN 1-85260-418-2

Patrick Stephens Limited is a member of the Haynes Publishing Group P.L.C., Sparkford, Nr Yeovil, Somerset, BA22 7JJ.

Printed and bound in Hong Kong.

CONTENTS

My last book, *Photographing Beautiful Women*, was very much a practical guide to techniques and marketing. While it was fun to put together, concentrating on the 'how to' aspects of my work didn't allow me much scope to address a rather more fundamental question: call it the 'why' aspect.

Specializing in taking pictures of the female form is not a passive career choice; I've yet to see a recruitment ad offering this line of work. So anyone like me who comes to earn their living this way must have made a conscious decision to do so. But as the years roll by and the jobs mount up, it becomes easy to get so immersed in day-to-day practicalities that there seems no time to look inwards.

In many respects, writing this book was an attempt to draw back and examine my life from a more detached viewpoint. I needed to ask myself that 'why?' question again, if you like.

The conclusions I came to were hardly earth-shattering, but they were important for me. On the most basic level, I decided that I was still photographing beautiful women because I enjoyed it more than anything else I could be doing. In spite of the commercial constraints imposed on much of my work, in spite of the pressures involved in running my own business, I continue to find something magical in capturing the infinite variety of the female form. That may sound pretentious, but it is the best way I can explain my motives for doing what I do.

Reading about my work, you might get the impression that often I am trapped in a formula, a style, imposed on me by my clients. But the creative kick for me is to transcend those limitations, to explore the mystery and eroticism of woman in a way that satisfies me and yet still produce images which please my customers. As long as I continue to find that a challenge, I shall continue to look forward to my next shoot.

JANUARY

JANUARY

My birthday is on 31 December, which gives the start of a new year a sharper focus for me than for most people. Although I have to say that focusing generally takes a little while when I wake up on 1 January, as I traditionally throw a party on New Year's Eve – why is it that double celebrations mean you drink twice as much?

So it's normally in fairly subdued mood that I view the world of work at the beginning of the year. It's a time for taking stock, reflecting on what the previous 12 months have brought me, and seeing how they matched up to the hopes and fears I had when I went through the same exercise after my last birthday.

The one sure bet is that I won't have foreseen many of the triumphs and disasters, because working for yourself as a professional photographer teaches you to expect the unexpected. Work doesn't often walk through the door, I have to go out and get it. And, having got it, I have to come up with the goods. The marketplace has got tougher as money has got tighter, and there are more photographers chasing fewer jobs than there were when I started out in the seventies.

It's no good expecting to be able to just bumble along, you need to plan, you need to revise your thinking constantly. If all I had to do was get my pictures right, then life would be a lot easier, but don't forget that I'm running a business – the amount of time I actually spend behind a lens shooting is probably no more than a third of my working

month. The rest of the time I'm talking to clients, editing material I've already shot, doing the pre-production work for jobs I'm going to shoot, and organizing my office – there's no point in persuading a client to send you on an enjoyable working trip to the Caribbean if you come back to find that the Vatman or the Inland Revenue inspector has taken you to court for unpaid taxes in your absence, because you didn't get your paperwork together.

So, what am I planning this year? I'm planning to leave the studio I've had for 16 years in London's West End, that's probably the biggest single decision I've made. Not that I've been unhappy there, far from it. But the beginning of my chapter on the use of studios in my last book comes echoing back to me as I write this one six years later: 'The first point to emphasize about studios is that you don't need one. Many photographers who concentrate on shooting for the magazine, library and calendar market shoot the vast majority of their work on location, and rightly say that they can't justify the high running costs of maintaining a permanent studio.'

That sums up my situation exactly. When I wrote those words I was doing a lot of jobs – mainly for fashion and advertising – which involved building complicated and sizeable studio sets. Times and styles have changed, though. One of the trends of last year was that fewer and fewer of my clients were demanding that kind of work, while my overheads to run the place rocketed. My studio is gradually changing from a faithful friend into a demanding mistress, and it's time to move on.

JANUARY

Where to go, is the question. I'm going to have to do some hard thinking this month.

Meanwhile, the show goes on. Looking forward, what work do I see this month; this year? Some jobs, like the shoot I'm going to do later this week with Kirsten Imrie, one of my favourite models of all time, appear sharply defined, right slap bang in the foreground. Others, like a swimwear trip to the Caribbean for a regular client planned for the spring, beckon invitingly in the middle distance. And there will be other trips, but when, and where and for whom remains to be decided. So, for the moment, let's get on with organizing the Kirsten shoot.

The client is pleased. Not that I doubted for a minute he would be, because Kirsten is a joy to work with. Apart from a beautiful face and ravishing figure, she has a great personality. But, above all, she has the best skin I've ever seen. Every time I photograph her, and it's been quite a number now, I rave about the way her skin lights so well – it glows. I must stop going on about it, though, because my intrepid assistant Jane and Claire, the make-up artist I normally use, are beginning to get severely bored with me. I did it again on this shoot, the words just slipped out, and were greeted with a chorus of: 'Oh, no! Not again!' and mimes of throwing up in a bucket. I got my own back, though – I grabbed my mobile phone, snuck into the reception area and phoned Claire's mobile.

I heard her scamper over to the dressing-room to grab the phone. When she answered, I said brightly: 'You know, Kirsten's skin really loves the light,' then hung up quickly, although not before the make-up artist had invited me to perform a biologically improbable act!

****

15

JANUARY

Into the fourth week in January, and I've spent precisely two days shooting in the studio. This makes me more determined than ever to get off my backside and do something about moving. It's not that I haven't been working; if anything, work's been brisker than I expected, certainly brisker than it was 12 months ago. But it's been practically all on location. Nowhere exotic, alas, unless you count Canterbury and West London as exotic. Still, the point is I've got to the stage where I can hire a decent indoor location, any one of dozens of houses all with different styles and decor, for far less than it costs me to build and hire props for an equivalent room set in my studio, if you add the studio overheads into the equation. A rent review looms – perhaps that will concentrate my mind.

******

This week is also glasnost week, because I've spent some time shooting two Eastern European models. Although only about 25 per cent of my work these days is for men's magazines, I have to be constantly on the lookout for fresh models for them. While advertising and calendar clients tend to favour professional models from the established agencies, men's magazines shy away from girls who've had too much exposure, in every sense of the word. Half the battle is to tempt them with girls who've not appeared in any rival publica-

tions. And that ain't easy, because all my competitors are also scouring the countryside for new talent.

This source looks promising though, thanks to Anya, a Czechoslovakian girl who had the enterprise to navigate herself to London in the eighties, and worked happily and profitably as a model for several years. Having seen the potential for work in the UK, she went back home and set about establishing her own agency, and now comes over regularly with two or three girls at a time. When she's planning a

trip she sends me test pictures of any new girls she has on her books beforehand, and I phone her up and book the ones I think are right for the market.

Obviously, she deals with other photographers as well, but she's sensible about telling each of us what other arrangements she's made. I say sensible, because nothing makes me madder than to spend time and money on a speculative magazine shoot, offer the pictures to an editor who normally laps up my work, only to get a rejection because he's just bought a set of pictures of the same girl from another photographer. Models are not always the most reliable witnesses when it comes to telling you what work they've done recently. They have a natural desire to do as much work as possible, and are unlikely to say anything they think might lose them a job. In fairness, too, they don't always know when doing a session where the pictures are likely to end up.

Good agents, though, realize that if they want repeat business they must be honest with photographers. It's a small enough world, the glamour world, and word quickly gets round if anyone is trying to pull a fast one. Bookings soon die off.

****

It was next stop Italy for Anya and the girls, where again they would be fresh faces and therefore in demand. Anya said she wouldn't be back in England for several months, so I have to start thinking about where my next magazine models are coming from. I have various contacts: make-up artists often recommend me to models they've worked with on other jobs, models recommend other models, and up and down the country there are smaller agencies who keep in touch. But the timing isn't always right for me with these occasional sources. If a girl is keen to work and comes to see me just before I'm off on a trip, chances are she'll have been in touch with a number of other photographers and been photographed before I get back.

One answer I'm toying with is to reverse the equation – instead of waiting for new models to come to me, I'll go out and find them. America looks the best bet, on several fronts. I've worked there a number of times on commissioned shoots, mainly in California and Florida, and have contacts there. In these days of sky wars, when airlines are offering cut-throat rates just to get bums on their plane seats rather than those of their competitors, the cost of getting out there is reasonable; the light can be tremendous; and I don't have a language barrier to contend with (well, not much of one, anyway). Could be something to consider for the autumn.

We'll see!

The model hunt goes on. For the last few years I've spent three or four days each February making sure I'm up to date with the agency scene, keeping tabs on the talent available. Call it stocktaking, if you like.

The way it works is that I contact all the major London agencies and arrange appointments for the girls that I've seen in their current model books I think might be suitable for future work, plus any new signings they've made since publishing their books. I work on the basis of around 10 minutes a girl – I have a brief chat, look through their portfolios, and then put them on video for future reference. It might not sound the worst job in the world – asking 100 or more models to step into your studio and out of their clothes – but a non-stop diet of anything can get pretty tedious after a while. Sometimes it reminds me of those London apprentices a couple of centuries ago who complained that they were being given salmon every lunchtime.

This year I saw 120 girls in three days, and out of those, perhaps 25 or so look promising. I'm looking mainly for models suitable for calendar work at the moment, because later in the month I've got to sit down with Moments, a calendar company I shoot for regularly on commission, and plan our strategy for the year. I'm also trying to expand my library of calendar shots, as Dave Muscroft, the energetic guy who markets my library material, has convinced me that this is a growth area at the moment.

That's all very well, but it doesn't help the cash flow. I have to lay out all the expenses up front when I'm doing speculative shoots – the models, the make-up artist, the location owner if I'm not shooting in the studio, all expect to get paid promptly, while the money from library sales trickles in over months, sometimes years. It's a delicate balance between current expenditure and future earnings, as the studio continues to gobble up money.

******

Bad news. My Caribbean brochure swimwear trip in the spring is off. This is something I could do without, especially as the cancellation is so unexpected. I did the equivalent shoot for them last year, everybody was happy with the shots: and now this. I seem to be the victim of an internal power struggle – the firm's parent company changed hands, and the swimwear people were suddenly working for new masters who have brought in their own advertising agency. On this type of job the photographer is generally hired by the creative director of the ad agency involved, and each creative director has his own favourite sons. So, new agency, new photographer. Simple as that.

Understanding the reasons doesn't make me any happier, though. It's less than a month's notice, for one thing, and I've turned down other jobs for those three weeks. Plus I've already put a lot of creative effort into the job, what with casting sessions, discussions about the number of shots we were going to do, having preliminary thoughts about what styling would suit what garment, and so on. A hefty cancellation fee is in order here, but from their evasive initial reaction when I started talking money, this argument is going to go the distance. And all of a sudden I've got a big hole in the diary.

FEBRUARY

A New York photographer friend of mine has what he calls his Big Deal Jar. Whenever anyone contacts him to start discussing a possible job, he writes the name of the client on a piece of paper, wraps it around a dollar coin, and drops the coin into the jar. At the end of the year he dumps the contents of the jar on to his desk and separates off the jobs that actually happened from those that didn't. He reckons he usually has about $100 left over. But there's a big difference between a casual enquiry and the detailed discussions we've had on this one.

Still, those castings weren't a total waste, because one of the models I saw, Gloria, turned out to be just right for a speculative calendar shoot I did this week in Diana Dors' former house. The house itself isn't anything very special, but it has the most outrageous swimming pool, which I'd been dying to use as a location ever since I first saw pictures of it. The huge double doors are a riot of art deco stained glass, and the steps to the pool are guarded by two black stone panthers. Sliding glass patio doors take up the entire south-facing side of the room, letting in the sun. The whole scene is completely over the top, but very striking, and just right for Gloria's sultry charms. The shoot worked out very well, although the lighting was tricky – I had to put lights shining through the art deco door, light the pool separately to make it shine, and prevent the pool side areas becoming a dingy dead zone. Let's hope the pictures sell.

Matching style to location is important. Gloria's (fake) leopard-skin thong complements the tropical feel of the pool in the late Diana Dors' house

---

FEBRUARY

Discussions with Moments are going well, which helps dull the pain of the swimwear shambles. At least some of my regular clients are faithful. I've done a geat deal of work for Moments over the last six years, and fortunately their business seems to be going from strength to strength, they're about the biggest calendar company around now. They produce dozens of different calendars a year, with all sorts of themes – vintage cars, stately homes, village scenes and, of course, beautiful girls.

Ironically, they first got in touch with me because they wanted to buy subsidiary rights to a calendar I'd shot for someone else, a lingerie extravaganza I'd produced for the Bowater company. I didn't have the rights to those pictures, which in a sense was fortunate, because a little while later Moments came back to me and said: 'What would you charge to shoot a calendar specifically for us?' We discussed the styling, hammered out a deal, I shot a calendar for them entitled *Girls at Home*, and I've been working for them ever since.

They've pleasantly surprised me this year by suggesting I shoot no less than three separate calendars, which is one more than I'd expected. The idea is one atmospheric studio-based production – very stark, with minimal propping, concentrating on body shapes; one country number – plenty of fields and flowers, that

The gilt factor on this chaise longue gives this studio shot of Petra an air of ritzy elegance

type of thing; and another bedroom-based *Girls at Home* production. So, now I can get on and start thinking about locations, models and timing. It would be handy to do one in March, to fill in the gap that's appeared, but I don't think I'm going to be able to get it organized in time, because I'll need client approval on every aspect of the jobs before I can go ahead: budget, models and locations being the main items.

FEBRUARY

I've heard of a location that might be ideal for the bedroom material – a large country house near Norwich, somewhere that has at least a dozen bedrooms, all with different themes. So I think I'll go and check that one out next week.

****

Instead of East Anglia, Les Arcs. Pleasant surprise number two of the month. Peugeot – bikes, not cars – flew me out to the French ski resort to photograph their mountain bike range. Not a girl in sight in my pictures for a change, but a bunch of muscly cyclists whizzing up and down the slopes.

I'd rarely photographed in snow before, but I knew that the conditions would throw the automatic metering of my Nikon F3 into confusion. Meters measure light against an average shade of grey, and just can't cope with vast expanses of white, because they adjust to such a radical deviation from the norm. If you let the meter make the decision, all your pictures will turn out underexposed. Aware of the problem, I overrode the meter by a couple of stops, and all the shots turned out spot on. Certainly a great deal more professional than my first attempts at skiing.

Bathrooms can make excellent locations, but space is usually a problem. The setting of this Moments calendar test picture of Jade is a welcome exception

****

Choose your angles and lighting positions carefully when shooting into windows to avoid reflections which could cause flare

FEBRUARY

Two days to go to March. I haven't managed to find a commission to replace the Caribbean trip, but I must keep busy, so I've decided to put together a speculative location package. I went up to check out Gunthorpe Hall, the East Anglian location I had marked down as a possibility for Moments, and it's ideal for what I have in mind: seven days, six models, and just as much calendar and magazine material as I can pack in. It'll be a sweat but, with luck, a profitable sweat. I've spent the last few days sorting out the models, and while at this short notice I wasn't able to book all my first choices, I think I've assembled a reasonable bunch.

In between organizing that shoot, I've also been taking some pictures for my own pleasure. That may sound a bit of a busman's holiday, but it has a practical side to it as well. I usually can't afford to experiment too much when I'm shooting commercially, because I have to keep my eyes firmly on the market I'm aiming at, and those markets are basically conservative – their general atitude can be summed up as: 'Love what you did last time – more of the same, please.'

But without experimentation you're never going to progress, you're going to get stuck in a groove. This doesn't bother some glamour photographers – they carry on churning out work on a production-line basis. That's not good enough for me, though. While we all need to make a living, I chose this business because I thought I had something to offer creatively, and I still feel that way. Some of my ideas may turn out to be duds, others may produce results that please me but have no practical application. It doesn't matter, at least I've had a go. When it comes to lighting, lenses and locations, I'll try anything once.

And while, as I've said, most clients are inclined to play safe if in doubt, they can sometimes be persuaded to look at a job in a different way. I find the most satisfying jobs are often those when I've been hired as much for my creative input as for my technical ability. Say I've been asked to pitch for a fashion shoot; what I enjoy most is a client who says: 'We've got these garments to photograph: how do you suggest we do it?'

While obviously there will be constraints of time and money, that's part of the challenge, and if I suggest a certain style or technique, I'm in a much stronger position if I can back up my ideas with a visual reference from my portfolio. And these references will often be precisely those photographs I've taken while experimenting.

Wendy (below) and Tina modelled for these experimental pictures in return for some shots for their own portfolios

---

MARCH

*Cover girl Emma takes her ease on
my favourite four-poster*

MARCH

Half-way through the Gunthorpe week, and it's working well. And I'm working well. Getting out of London at this time of year is no bad thing, and although you couldn't accuse East Anglia of being anything less than very cold, I like the area, and I like the big skies. When the north wind blows you can tell there's nothing higher than a chimney stack separating this part of the world from the Arctic, but as I'm not daft enough to contemplate shooting out of doors at this time of year, it only affects me when I'm getting in and out of the car as I ferry each day's model to and from Norwich station.

I'm working on a tight schedule; six days, seven models, all of whom are coming up from London – early train in, last train back. It's a 30-mile round trip to Norwich, and in past years that kind of running around would have been the job of my assistant. But Jane has a photographic commission of her own to shoot in the studio this week, as she continues her transition from an assistant to a photographer in her own right, and I'm happy for the studio to be used, even if it means more work for me.

In fact, I find myself doing without Jane's assistance more and more. Not because I think she's not up to it – quite the reverse. But I'm travelling lighter these days, stripping away some of the excess baggage of my working life. (Not that I mean to suggest Jane herself is either excessive or a baggage, of course!)

Every photographer has a different attitude towards assistants. Some, including several very well-known names, get their assistants to do practically all the donkey work on a shoot, enabling the photographer to breeze in at the last minute and get behind the lens without having had any of the drudgery.

That's not my style – I like to get my hands dirty, if you like. I want to do my own lighting, I want to play an active part in styling the set, choosing the props. It may be partly arrogance on my part, a feeling that I know better than anyone else, but I like to be in control. After all, it's my reputation, my livelihood, that's at stake.

When I was building a lot of studio room sets and shooting far more medium-format work than I do now, an assistant was a necessity rather than a luxury. He or she – and over the years I've employed more she's than he's – would help build and break

down the sets, keep the studio tidy, run around town tracking down props, load film (essential when I was shooting with a medium-format camera like a Hasselblad), and generally have a busy time of it.

Now I work far less in the studio and shoot almost exclusively 35mm, there just isn't the work to keep an assistant employed all day every day, which is why I'm so lucky with Jane. When I really need her, she's there, but when I don't, she gets on with planning her own career, just as I did when I was an ambitious young assistant. The arrangement works well. We make a good team.

So, I'm organizing myself at Gunthorpe. I'm not completely without help, because Claire is with me for the week to do the make-up – that's one area I'm not arrogant enough to assume I can cope with myself – and helps me in other ways, such as keeping me fuelled with constant cups of coffee. The more I work in the house, the more I like it. Still being restored, it's the pet project of an American woman who used to be a photographic assistant herself, working for Hank Londoner, a leading New York fashion photographer. She and her English husband are intent on restoring Gunthorpe to its former glory, and they've certainly got plenty of work on their hands – the estate must be 100 acres at least, with a farm, cottages, outbuildings and a large lake, as well as the main house which has got a dozen or more bedrooms.

MARCH

Not that I'm using them all. Deciding what to leave out of a picture is just as important as deciding what to include. The temptation is often to try to feature every detail of a location – to get your money's worth, as it were. That is usually a mistake, because it is fatal to allow the set to dominate the picture. You must always remember that you're photographing a beautiful girl, not producing a furniture catalogue.

For instance, there's one room at Gunthorpe I'm particularly taken with. It's large, so I'm not tripping over my lights all the time, and its main feature is a huge four-poster bed. I shall probably have used it for several sessions before I'm done. By changing the model, the clothes, the bedding and whatever props I keep in shot, plus subtly altering the lighting each time, I'm confident I can create a completely different mood each time. While

I'll use other rooms as well, what I want to do is avoid room-hopping relentlessly, like some oversexed guest at an Edwardian country house weekend. Every change of room will involve me in stripping down my lights and setting them up again, and this week time is money in a very real sense. Without compromising quality, I want to return with as much marketable material as I possibly can.

Back home late on Saturday, shattered. It's been a hard week. Glamour photography is a very physical activity – there are weighty flashpacks and lights to hump around, often furniture to be moved, and you're also on your feet all day. At Gunthorpe I was getting up at 6.30 in the morning, and it was usually around 9 at night before I finally slumped on to a barstool for a reviving drink after the model run to Norwich.

I'm going to spend tomorrow reminding the family who I am, and then on Monday I think I deserve a round of golf after I've taken all my film into the lab to be processed. Anyway, whether I deserve it or not, I'm going to have one.

Maria looks straight at camera for a calendar picture, but conveys a more tranquil mood for a one-off magazine illustration

MARCH

I'm busy editing the Gunthorpe pictures and arranging them in clear viewing sleeves. Shooting a job is only half the battle, I then need to pull out the best pictures from each session, because I always shoot more frames than are ever going to be used. This isn't self-indulgence, it makes good business sense the way I work. When I'm shooting I don't work to a rigid, preconceived plan. I try to build up a rapport with the model, and if the session is going well she'll be constantly changing poses, altering her body shapes. I always encourage my models to be active participants in the shoot rather than lying back passively, waiting to be told by me what to do. Some models are better at this than others, of course – some have an intuitive feel for what I'm trying to achieve. I'm happiest when a session takes on a life of its own as it progresses, and I end up exploring angles and approaches that hadn't occurred to me before I picked up the camera. A slight shift of a leg here, a turn of the head there, can make the difference betwen an average shot and an outstanding one.

So, it's foolish to economize on film and processing, because, when balanced against the other expenses of any shoot, they are a relatively small part of the equation.

I tend to shoot all my glamour material on Fuji film stock these days. In the old days, everyone insisted on Kodachrome for 35mm work, because at the time it was one of the few films that had no grain, and 35 mm transparencies could be greatly enlarged without any noticeable loss of quality.

That was all very well, but it was also limiting for me, because I found that to guarantee the exact exposure I wanted I was forced to bracket, to shoot on the light and dark side of what I thought was the correct exposure. As I mentioned, talking about Les Arcs, a light meter is only reliable within certain tolerances. Working this way made for a slower pace of shooting, and the need to cover myself sometimes meant that I didn't achieve that momentum I find so rewarding.

Now I find the new Fuji emulsions give me equally good results – better in some cases. Fuji 50, filtered correctly, produces excellent flesh tones, with the punchy colour saturation I'm looking for. It is also far more flexible than Kodachrome at the processing stage. Using Kodachrome I had to send the film off to Kodak for processing, and had no control of the finished result. With Fuji film I can take it to my preferred processing lab and get them to do a clip test, which involves processing a short length of each roll. I can look at these and decide whether I like the colour quality or not. If I don't, the lab can alter the colour density of the rest of the roll to my specifications.

All of which means that just about every frame I shoot these days is usable, in terms of technical quality at any rate. As none of the clients I syndicate to will accept duplicate transparencies these days, on account of the perceptible loss of quality, it means that at any one time I can have far more material doing the rounds, being considered for purchase, than I could in my Kodachrome days.

APRIL

This morning, dear old Auntie BBC broadcast one of her ponderous April Fool's Day spoofs, claiming that scientists have isolated a humour gene in the human body. If it were true, I can think of one or two people who are a gene short of the full set. I've been wrangling with the swimwear people who cancelled me out at the last minute, and the bottom line is that they're prepared to pay me for all the pre-production work I did, but refuse to cough up a cancellation fee. As there was nothing down on paper, there's not a lot I can do but grin and bear it; getting my own humour gene working at full stretch.

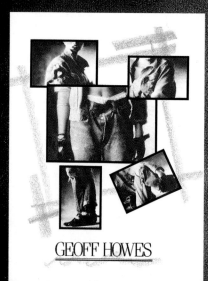

GEOFF HOWES

APRIL

It's also time to put myself about a bit more, keep my name uppermost in the minds of creative directors and commissioning editors. Some photographers delegate that aspect of the business entirely, preferring to have an agent to represent them. The agent will make appointments with advertising agencies and magazines, generally hawking their clients' portfolios around town, and take a percentage commission from any work they drum up.

A few photographers have an agent who represents them exclusively, but you have to be turning over an awful lot of money to make that an economic proposition. The more normal set-up is for the agent to represent several photographers who have clearly defined and mutually exclusive areas of interest and expertise: still life, cars, glamour, say.

In the past, I've been this route myself. I had an agent for a while and, yes, she did indeed get me some work. But it wasn't a totally satisfactory arrangement, because by that time I'd already been working for a number of years, and I wanted to continue dealing direct with my existing clients. More to the point, they expected to carry on dealing directly with me, they would have been slightly insulted at suddenly having a middleman – or in my case, middlewoman – intruding into the action.

So now I again handle all the client contact myself and, while I know that I must miss out on certain jobs because neither I nor someone representing me was around to discuss them when they were up for grabs, I have to balance that against the fact that I'm not having to fork out 25 per cent of the take to someone else. But there are ways to promote yourself that don't involve cold-calling prospective clients, and one of these is to mail out a promotional poster each year.

The idea is to produce something so appealing that it will get stuck up on the wall of the potential and existing clients you send it to, keeping your name constantly on display. I've got a photo-montage concept I've been tinkering with, in fact I've more or less designed it in my head. Perhaps now is the time to get it done.

****

The poster's turned out very well. Whether it gets me any more work remains to be seen, but it was fun to shoot. I started off by approaching a fashion model agency, asking if any of their girls wanted test shots for their portfolios, and had no problem finding a taker, because it's a deal which benefits both parties. No money changes hands; the model gives me her time, I cover all the shooting expenses and give her a selection of the resulting pictures for her portfolio. That way, both of you end up with more work to market yourself with.

The same principle applied to a swimwear shot I've done this week. For reasons too painful to go into again, I've been thinking my portfolio is a little light on the swimwear front, so when Efua, a model I worked with on a fashion assignment last year, popped into the studio to remind me she was still in the market for work, it seemed a good idea to take advantage of the opportunity and put something together on the spur of the moment. She'd got into body building in a big way, so her body, though still curvy, had an athlete's muscle definition, and the steamy, sweaty feel of the styling seemed appropriate.

This version of my poster girl demonstrates how contrast is reduced by shooting in colour as opposed to black and white

A quarter of the way through the year, it's time to take stock of where I'm heading; as far as that's possible in this rackety business. I've drawn up three lists: one of definite work; one of possible work – work I'm going to hustle for, work I'd like to get; and one of speculative shoots I plan to organize myself, because I'm confident I'll be able to sell the material.

Of the definites, Moments is still top of the list. We've been discussing the three calendars in more detail, and revised our thinking somewhat. The plan now is for me to shoot the *Girls at Home* calendar over the spring and summer as a series of one-off sessions, fitting those in around my other work. The outdoor calendar, *Visions*, we'll do in one go on location, probably abroad, to cut down the risk of bad weather; and *Reflections*, the studio-based one, can be fitted in any time before October.

Other definites, although how many jobs it's impossible to quantify, include several days' work a month for three or four regular fashion and advertising clients. These tend to be last-minute affairs, calling for a quick turnround, so they're difficult to build into my planning.

The 'possible work' list includes two other calendars I'm pitching for. They'll be one-offs for individual companies rather than calendar specialists like Moments. In the past, I've done a number of these, for firms like Bowater, British Airways and the like, but the market is shrinking – they're an expensive form of corporate advertising, exactly the kind of project companies cut down or abandon when times get tough financially.

Mixing styles can be effective, as in this blend of fifties-style make-up and modern technique

45

*Few locations are perfect.
The bedrail in this otherwise
brilliant room caused me problems
with angles, until I discovered it
could be removed*

APRIL

Back to one of my favourite locations, a rambling old manor house just outside Canterbury, for a magazine shoot. I've been coming here for four years now, and I must be careful not to overdo it. But it's not as though I'm always shooting for the same markets here.

The owners, Ted and Jenny, are one of the attractions. They always dish up a good lunch, and keep me and the models supplied with coffee and biscuits during the day, without ever being obtrusive. It's not just laziness, though, that brings me back here. I've moved steadily towards simpler settings over the years, away from the more fussy, cluttered look I once favoured, and the bedroom I always use here is ideal, and has a nice ambience.

The advantage of returning to a location is that you know exactly what lighting set-up to use. Because you've already worked out various angles and positions on previous visits, you don't have to start from scratch. And this room is unusually long, it runs from front to back of the house, which allows me to position the camera well away from the bed.

The first time I shot there the bedrail at the foot of the bed gave me some problems, because to avoid it intruding into the shot I was forced into some curious angles. It wasn't until my third visit that I realized that by uscrewing the bedknobs, I could remove the entire rail, which gave me a lot more flexibility. It also took me a couple of visits to stop smashing my head against the ceiling beams – the bedroom was in the eaves of a barn conversion, and if you're over six foot like me, a close encounter with a 5ft 6in beam is painful, believe me.

****

Jane, the model I'm working with today, has given me an idea. As she chatted away while we were shooting, she told me her agency is in the process of setting up a trip to the Mediterranean for

amateur photographers. They've advertised in the photographic magazines and got over 20 takers so far, so their plan is to take five models, plus a professional photographer to advise and give lectures on technique, to Kos, one of the larger Greek islands, sometime in the spring.

What I'm thinking is that, if the models are good enough, it might be worth my while doing a deal with the agency and tacking myself on to the trip. I haven't shot any outdoor material since last autumn, and this way all I would have to fund are my own flight and expenses, plus model fees.

I'll give the agency a call, and find out more.

Changes of outfit during a session produce a varied product which maximizes sales potential

I was probably a little over-ambitious on my Gunthorpe Hall trip. Looking back over the pictures, I can see where tiredness set in at the end of the week. There's one set I'm having great difficulty in selling, and to be honest I can see why – the model I used on the last day just wasn't up to scratch. Lovely figure, sure, but also a cold sore of dramatic proportions on her upper lip. Needless to say, neither she nor her agency had bothered to mention this trifling detail, but I remember my heart sinking when I picked her up from the station. I could swear I could see that sore pulsating, it seemed to have a life of its own.

If I'd had any sense I should have been more hard-hearted at the time, told her that I didn't think it was on to turn up looking like that, and sent her packing on the next train back to London. But what would I have done the rest of the day? Packed up and gone home early, would have been the best answer, but instead, I asked Claire to do her best to rescue the situation with plenty of make-up. Trouble was, she had to plaster so much on I'm surprised it didn't crack.

Little Miss X – the name has been changed to protect the guilty – had a slightly haughty, horsey look, which can be quite

erotic if handled properly, but the poor girl was obviously suffering from her cold, and I'm afraid it shows. It's obvious in every frame that she isn't enjoying herself. And any hint of boredom or sulleness in a model is the ultimate turn-off. Whoever said: 'The camera does not lie' was a fool, it lies all the time. But even my faithful Nikon couldn't get away with a whopper like this. I might just as well put the pictures straight in the bin.

****

There's no point in looking back in anger, though. Apart from anything else, I haven't got the time, because I've got to crack on with organizing *Girls at Home*, the first of my trio of Moments calendars for the year. In many ways it's the most difficult one to shoot, because it's had a chequered history. The basic concept is simple enough: six pages, each featuring a different girl, with one dominant picture and two or three smaller, drop-in shots. Each year, though, the style has changed as the thinking of the Moments people has changed.

I got the job originally because Moments liked my work on the Bowater calendar, so the brief was: 'More of the same, please'. Previous *Girls at Home* calendars had been very breezy and obvious in their styling. Subtlety wasn't their strong point, and they were almost cheesecakey, with the slightly dated air that word implies.

I'd shot the Bowater calendar in a stately home called Brocket Hall, and for my first *Girls at Home* I used similarly opulent locations. While I'm not unhappy with the shots, I no longer favour quite such palatial settings, because I think the danger is that they divert attention away from the model – I want people to admire the female, not the furniture.

There's also a slight credibility gap between the title *Girls at Home* and such settings. I'm not suggesting we should have used suburban semis as locations, but since remarkably few girls actually live in stately piles like these, the image is wrong. One of these days a duke's curvy young daughter might invite me to come and photograph her as she slips into something silky after a hard morning out with the hunt, but it hasn't happened yet.

So, over the years the brief has changed. In consultation with Moments, who put a great deal of effort into *Girls at Home* because it's one of their biggest sellers, I've throttled back on the luxurious locations, and altered the styling. In place of the very romantic, soft-focus feel of my earlier productions, I've concentrated on developing a more understated mood, and attempted to inject an air of slight mystery. Who is this girl? What is she thinking? What is her life?

One of the principal methods I've used to try to achieve this mood is lighting. Instead of having an overly bright set I put one light source on the model, and use a big softbox to separate off the background with a warm, diffused glow. Plenty of shadow tends to draw the eye to the model rather than the set.

Tracey Elvick's principal claim to fame is her Page Three appearances, but she still finds time for calendar work

The romanticizing effect of soft focus allowed me to pose Anneleise in a way that would otherwise have been too brash and obvious

---

MAY

The point about all this is that each change of emphasis over the years has been the outcome of long discussions with Moments. On one level, the client is always right, but it isn't as simple as that in most cases, because the client is often looking to you for creative input. On some jobs, the easiest part is actually taking the photographs – the hard work has been deciding what photographs to take.

I can't stand wasting my time and effort because the client's indecision is final. I hate the kind of job where the client or art director starts messing me about in the middle of shooting, when as far as I'm concerned we've agreed exactly what we're up to.

I did a fashion catalogue shoot earlier this month which drove me barmy. Before we started we'd agreed an exact format, to the extent of producing visuals (drawings of each shot) and a layout for all the pages.

But on the very first shot the client suddenly started overriding his art director, asking me to alter everything in mid-shoot, because he didn't know what he wanted until he saw it. In the end I had to put my foot down, because we were taking far too long on each set-up; I was shooting every picture three times, and the job was in danger of spilling over into another day, with all the extra costs that would entail. I also felt I was being forced to do three times the work I was being paid for, because I was on a fee rather than a day rate, and if through no fault of my own it took me a week rather than a day to complete the job, I could foresee a hassle negotiating what I regarded as a fair increase for all the extra work.

A sensible client will always be guided by his creative team, because there's no point in having a dog and barking yourself. Any art director worth his salt will know the art of the possible – what is achievable and what isn't.

One simple prop adds volumes to the mood of this deserted ballroom scene featuring Sandra-Jane

MAY

Having said all that, it's not an ideal world – occasionally things can, and do, go wrong. The most nerve-racking times are when, having made your plans, you start shooting and realize that the concept just isn't working.

Lack of time is usually the culprit when accidents are looking for somewhere to happen. The last time I got caught out was with an advertising job for one of the sponsors of the London to Brighton cycle race. It was literally an overnight affair –

I was briefed over the phone one morning, with the shoot scheduled for the studio the following day.

The shot was to feature the classic nuclear family – mother, father, two kids, cycling along a caricature roadway, complete with fake hedgerow in the background. I knocked up the set in record time, giving it as much width as I could, because the clients had specified a horizontal picture.

Normally on an advertising job like this I'll be given an exact design to work to from the start, but there was no time for that. So, while I was slaving away feverishly with hammer, nails and paintbrush, the ad agency was writing the text and producing a layout.

Only drawback was, when the agency art director arrived the next morning clutching the layout, it was immediately obvious that my set was the wrong shape. Hard as I'd tried, it was nowhere near wide enough. With the 'family' arriving in three hours, I had to undertake a major reconstruction job. I didn't have a hope of knocking the entire set down and starting again in that time, so I decided the only way forward was to raise my fake road two feet off the ground, making it stable enough to support the weight of four people on bikes.

'Come on, let's go to the pub,' I said to the art director. His face darkened, but he tagged along, and when instead of ordering a large Scotch I negotiated the loan of a stack of beer crates, he began to see my point. We were just sliding the last crate into position as the models arrived, and the job got done.

******

Stately home locations can be overpowering unless used carefully, but the size of the rooms makes for more flexibility when shooting, as this master bedroom in a hunting lodge indicates

Suzanne Mizzi, one of the all-time Page Three greats, was a calendar favourite of mine until she gave up photographic work

MAY

The Kos trip is definitely on. The agency sent me videos of the five models they're taking, and they look usable. My plan is to shoot a mixed bag of speculative material for Dave Muscroft to market – magazine sets, one-off calendar pictures and headshots. He's a grafter, Dave, he doesn't sit back and wait for the markets to come to him, he goes out and pursues sales. He's forever nagging me to produce more material, and has just come up with an offer to bankroll my production costs on speculative shoots in an effort to try to get me to step up my work-rate.

I could shoot more, I suppose.

I certainly don't regard myself as lazy, but handling most of the financial and production side of my business occupies a great deal of my time. Take a magazine shoot, for instance. In the seventies, magazines such as *Penthouse* took a far more active role in organizing the pictures they published. While they did buy in material which had been done on spec – the first glamour

64

pictures I ever sold, of a girl I'd met by chance at a party, were bought by *Penthouse* – the leading magazines would often plan their showcase pictorials themselves in every detail, and then hire a photographer to shoot them.

But in those days the economics of glamour photography were far kinder. A couple of decades on, the costs have risen far more steeply than the rewards. The magazine market is far more competitive, with many more titles around than ever before. Staffing levels have been pared to the bone, and editors don't have the resources they once enjoyed. It makes more sense for them to buy in a finished product than to get involved in the production process themselves.

So these days I do most of the pre-production work myself; I select and book the model, the location, and the make-up artist, decide on the styling, and gather together any props and clothing I'll need, although I admit that in this last area I do get a great deal of help from Jane.

And, another sign of the times, I'll shoot two sets of the same girl in a day, changing the clothing, styling and mood to produce two distinctly differing end products. In the past, it would never have occurred to me to aim for more than one set from a day's shoot, but those happy days are gone, I'm afraid. The figures just don't add up that way any more. It has to be rather more of a production line.

****

MAY

As a rough rule of thumb, I expect to clear the production costs with the first sale in the UK, and put the proceeds from the sale of the second set towards my overheads. So, at that stage I'm not making a profit – that has to come from the syndicated sales generated by Dave Muscroft and my other two agents around the world.

But at least I'm not out of pocket, because I have a very good percentage strike rate with magazine sales over here – cold sores permitting, of course. I shoot each set with a very firm idea of the outlet I'm aiming at. I know the preferences of each of the editors in terms of style, and keep in close contact with them to make sure I don't use models they've just bought pictures of from someone else.

Above all, though, I try to keep the quality high. Although ultimately the market is a finite one, I could do a lot more magazine work than the 30 or so sets a year I'm producing at the moment. But I'm sure I'd start to get stale and repetitive, and I like the variety my other work gives me.

Which takes me back to Dave Muscroft's suggestion, because while I enjoy the other speculative work he keeps pestering me to do, I don't have an immediate market for it in the way that I do for my magazine material. But if he's confident enough to fund speculative calendar and magazine cover shoots because he's sure my work is good enough to generate sales, then I'm happy to build them into my work pattern. It's always nice to be wanted. This way he gets more material from me, and I'm guaranteed a steady flow of working capital. There may be a catch somewhere, but I can't see it.

Minimal lighting on the model creates a moody, ethereal feel in these calendar pictures of Kathy and Laura

J U N E

The first in-flight drink is just slipping down my throat as we head off from Gatwick on our way to Kos. I enjoy trips – I've been on dozens and dozens over the years, but I still get a buzz from the planning and the anticipation. Mind you, it was a fair old shambles at the airport as 30 people, most of whom had never met before, milled around trying to make contact with each other.

Now what we want is good weather. I've been monitoring the forecasts for Greece over the last few days, and it's been changeable. I've long given up trying to shoot outdoors in Britain, because I can't guarantee the sun – it would be very frustrating to fly over 1,000 miles and have the same problem.

******

Two days into the fortnight, and the weather hasn't been at all changeable – it's been consistently grey and drizzly. At this rate, the main benefit I'm going to get from Kos is a distinct improvement in my snooker. The punters – sorry, the amateurs – are beginning to champ at the bit. They're a mixed bunch, ranging from teenagers to pensioners. Some have brought wives or girlfriends, obviously viewing the trip as much as a holiday as any kind of educational experience, but one or two of them are pretty intense char-

acters, who are here to take pictures and refuse to let the weather interfere with their plans. In between showers, they've been persuading the models outside and snapping their shutters in lighting conditions no professional in his right mind would ever attempt to work in.

Ralph, the professional contracted to hold their hands and talk them through the wonderful world of glamour photography, is doing his best, and trying to organize some indoor sessions, but we're all getting rather frustrated. Not least me, because in every other respect I think I've done an excellent deal. In return for helping out a bit with the amateurs – and I was pleased to see that a few of them have brought copies of my first book along with them – I've negotiated a distinctly family price for the model fees. After all, the girls are out here anyway, being paid by the agency, so any money on top is a bonus for them.

Model fees are always an important part of my budget, and costs vary depending on the type of job I'm doing. Fashion and advertising rates are always the highest, and in the past I've been quoted some silly money by agencies. We all know that the very top models – the superstars like Naomi Campbell and Linda Evangelista – earn hundreds of thousands of pounds a year. But that's the very small tip of the iceberg.

Last year, I was auditioning models for a 12-day fashion shoot in the West Indies, and was quoted a minimum of £2,000 a day for one of the girls I wanted to book. She was no superstar, just a good, sound professional, one of many. When I explained that the job was catalogue work, which traditionally commands a lower fee, the agency grudgingly dropped their price to £1,500. It just wasn't on at that figure, though – I had a total model budget of £3,500 for the trip, so I went and found another model whose agent wasn't living in dreamland.

It's vital when working with harsh sunlight and water that the models have a good, even suntan

JUNE

The drop in the amount of advertising work has forced some agents to see reason. These days, I'm paying around £500 a day for calendar models, and as little as half that for magazine models. When it comes to trips, I also expect the rate to reflect the fact that it's a guaranteed week's or fortnight's work somewhere pleasant – in other words, I'm looking for a healthy discount.

It surprises many people that glamour rates are at the lower end of the range – they seem to have the idea that the fewer clothes a model wears, the more she should earn. But it's really about professionalism, not prudery. Many of the models I shoot for magazines aren't in the business full-time, they're good-looking girls who are proud of their bodies and happy to show them off while earning some extra cash at the same time. Because they aren't full-time, though, they haven't benefited from the training and experience the professionals chalk up, and that can often make for slower working. An experienced model will know how to project her assets to the full, will work actively with the photographer to achieve the desired effect. Inexperienced models are more prone to ... well, to just lie there prone, waiting to be told what to do.

Beach and swimwear shoots demand lithe models with excellent muscle tone rather than soft, cushiony curves

JUNE

Day three, and the sun has got his hat on, hip, hip, hip hooray! Apart from exercising my cue arm, I've spent the last couple of days driving around and sniffing out locations, so now I'm off and running. Every day lost is money down the drain for me, but the deal for the amateurs when they're taking pictures is several of them to each model, so I won't have any problems of availability.

I've also had a chat with Ralph, who I've discovered is intending to do some work on his own account while he's out here as well. I didn't realize that before we arrived, and as he sells to the same markets as I do back in England, the situation could be a touch delicate. Fortunately, he shoots in a distinctively different style from mine. We've made a pact not to use the same settings, and agreed to liaise when it comes to sales, so that we don't both offer a set of the same girl to the same magazine at the same time. It's not ideal, but with goodwill on both sides it should work out ok.

The party has taken over an entire apartment complex, complete with gardens, tennis courts and swimming pool, so there won't be any problems of privacy. My plan initially is to shoot around the pool and on a couple of balconies that catch the sun at the right angles. As with my indoor work, these days I'm going more and more for simplicity out of doors as well. There are more than enough possibilities just around the pool – lilos, diving boards, showers, even hosepipes, are useful props. The slatted doors around the changing area could provide some scope, and even the white concrete walls can come into play, because I've noticed they are throwing up some interesting shadow effects.

Careful positioning of the model transforms this balcony location from an intrusive background into an actively helpful frame for the picture

This is no way to get a suntan, but going against logic can produce arresting images

JUNE

After that, I'll drive out to a couple of beaches I've found on my travels. It's not eactly miles-of-golden-sand time here, the beaches are small, but as most of my shots will be facing seawards, it doesn't honestly matter whether I've got ten feet or ten miles of seaside to play with.

What does matter is keeping out of the way of the amateurs while I'm shooting. Nothing personal, you understand, but I

find an audience is off-putting both for me and the model when I'm shooting for real. What I'll do for the amateurs is a couple of mock sessions without any film in the camera, explaining what lenses I'm using, what shapes I'm trying to achieve, what filters I feel will give me the best result with the light available. Already some of them have taken to coming up to me in the bar in the evenings with their work, asking for a critique. That's no hardship, I quite enjoy giving advice. I think it was George Bernard Shaw who said: 'Those who can, do, those who can't, teach.' All I

can say to the bearded bard is that it's pleasant to be able to do both.

But Ralph is bearing the brunt of the instruction, which is quite appropriate, because it wasn't that long ago that he was a happy amateur himself. In fact, he wasn't that happy, because at that time he had a full-time job in telecommunications that he detested. He'd been taking and selling a steady trickle of glamour pictures for a number of years, and one day he resolved to make the big break and turn his hobby into a way of earning a living. I admire him for that – it must be difficult to change careers completely in your late thirties.

There are a couple of amateurs on the trip who are keen to make the same progression. They've already sold material to magazines, and have come out here looking to polish their technique rather than learning the basics.

Wind can be an ally as well as an enemy. In Kos I had to slick the model's hair back with gel or water much of the time, but occasionally the wind worked to my advantage, as in the natural, unposed look I achieved here

JUNE

I'm quite touched by the attitude of most of the models towards the amateurs. I don't know quite what I'd expected – I thought perhaps the models might be a little blasé faced with a posse of beginners, and just go through the motions unenthusiastically. But if they're bored, they're not showing it. Perhaps this is because most models I've met have a well-developed exhibitionist streak to match their well-developed figures. They can't help playing to the camera, they're concerned to project themselves in the best way possible, even though they know that most of the pictures will never get published.

****

I had a long talk about studios with Ralph over dinner last night. His set-up sounds along the lines of what I'm looking for – he's got an office and a small studio in West London, in a building which houses a model agency and a couple of other companies. The rent is very reasonable, and includes all the facilities he needs – a receptionist to answer the phone and take messages when he's not there, a fax, secretarial services as and when he needs them.

While I've been out here I've been totting up what it costs me to run my studio, and the answer has horrified me – not far short of £50,000 a year. I've come to the conclusion that it's a bit like a Rolls Royce – if you have to ask whether you can afford one, the answer is probably no.

Ralph says the only drawback he finds in his place is a social one. He feels isolated. Once he's shut the door behind him in his set-up, he's totally on his own. There are times when that can be a blessing, of course, but as a steady diet it can be a rather solitary existence. He went on to say that there's another office adjoining his studio that will become vacant in a few weeks .... We didn't take the discussion any further than that, but I'm

certainly going to go and have a look at the place when I'm back in England.

****

The last day in Kos, and I think I've got enough material in the bag to have made it all worthwhile. The weather held for the rest of the fortnight – clear blue skies all the way after the first two days – and the models for the most part have come up with the goods. I think I probably did them down rather when I described them as merely 'usable', but until you start working with a girl you don't know how well she's going to work. Back home, it's rare for me

not to do test pictures before booking a model, so before I start shooting in earnest I have some idea of what to expect. In Kos, I was presented with five models selected by someone else, and although I'd seen them on video, that didn't tell me much except the basics of shape and colouring.

So, I'm pleased with the trip. As always, though, the proof of the pudding will be how much material I sell.

JUNE

'Borromei is an impressive yet homely manor house situated in the foothills of the Apuan Alps. The house is mainly eighteenth century but has parts dating back to the thirteenth century. It is eccentrically furnished, and many of the walls and ceilings are decorated with the original frescoes. Some of the rooms have fine antiques and old paintings, and the house has an air of faded elegance. The large garden, part-formal, part-natural, contains ancient urns and statues and has a delightful swimming pool in the woods, fed from a mountain spring.'

We'll take it. And at £1,150 for the week, the sun had better shine.

The location we've agreed on for *Visions*, my second Moments calendar of the year, is in Tuscany, what the author John Mortimer calls Chiantishire because of the number of ex-pat Brits who have settled there.

Why Tuscany? Well, why not? I've leafed through dozens of travel agents' brochures, and this place is closer than most to what I'm looking for in the way of variety of setting and ambience. Besides, I've never been to Tuscany.

Giving the model something to do gives variety to magazine sets, and in this case adds an air of unforced intimacy

JULY

The brief in Tuscany is quite clear-cut – we shouldn't have any London to Brighton cycle race-type dramas here. *Visions* is a 12 page production featuring four models, so it doesn't take a giant brain to work out that that makes three months for each of the girls. Each month will major on a single full-page shot, with one or two smaller drop-in pictures of the same girl in a different setting at Borromei.

I'm going to spend the first two days while I'm there having a thorough exploration of the location, working out individual shots. I will then compress the shooting into the next four days, leaving me a day spare as a fail-safe, and for packing up all the gear. When I'm working on location I get up early and put in long hours. This time I've mapped out a schedule of three hours' shooting a day with each model. So, it's quite a relaxed, leisurely itinerary for them, even adding on the time it will take to prepare their make-up; but it's a minimum 12-hour day for me!

I want this calendar to have a strong sense of place and to have a clear identity of its own; hence the single location. I need somewhere large enough to give me plenty of variety, both indoors and out; the split between the two is planned at roughly two thirds shot inside the house, and one third in and around the grounds.

I'm confident Borromei will offer me plenty of choice, because fortunately I haven't had to rely just on the brochure to get a flavour of the place; it was featured extensively in a recent copy of *Interiors* magazine. Having studied the 10-page spread of words and pictures they published, I feel I've learnt enough without having to go out there to do a preliminary recce; something I normally do on a major job like this. The first two days should be ample for that.

The line-up in Tuscany is going to be myself, Jane, Zeta doing make-up, the four models – Nikki, Karen, Angela and Helen – plus Chris and Steve from Moments. Jane and I are driving down in my shiny new Renault Espace with all my camera and lighting equipment, while the rest of them are flying to Pisa, which is just under 30 miles away. We're off in a fortnight's time, in the third week of July.

Couldn't be simpler. It always sounds so easy until you actually start shooting.

****

JULY

I went to see Ralph's studio in West London today, and it looks as good a set-up as it sounded when he was telling me about it in Kos. It's situated in a quiet little road, part offices, part residential. It's near a tube station, and – almost best of all – parking isn't a problem. I've lost count of the number of tickets I've collected over my years in the West End, because whenever I go on location I'm forced to bring the car into town to collect my equipment, and empty meter bays are non-existent in and around Bond Street.

I timed the run from my home near Hampton Court in Surrey to Ralph's place, and it was just under 40 minutes in fairly heavy traffic. I could cope with that.

Ralph introduced me to the guy who owns the building, Ken, who confirmed that the office space Ralph mentioned to me in Kos was indeed available. The package of office and shared studio with Ralph would cost me a quarter of what I'm paying now. The logic is overwhelming. The next step must be to find someone who wants to take over my existing lease, which may not be easy in the current depressed market.

Well, the gang's all here at Borromei. Not without a few dramas on the way, mind. Jane and I set off on our magical mystery tour by road nearly two days later than we'd intended, because of a delay in preparing our carnet. A carnet is an essential piece of documentation on large trips like this, when I'm lugging around equipment that collectively is worth not far short of £20,000. It is a form of bail bond, which lists every item of photographic equipment, and speeds up customs clearance no end. In countries where camera gear is more expensive than the UK, it's a guarantee that I haven't been flogging off bits and pieces to the natives. And when I return home, it's proof that I'm only coming back with what I went out with, and haven't been buying up goodies in duty-free areas.

Obviously, the system only works if the listing is 100 per cent accurate, and unfortunately the first list prepared for me contained some inaccuracies. I thought for a few seconds of trying to busk it, but I've had hang-ups at customs before when my paperwork hasn't been in order, and I couldn't face that prospect again. So I gritted my teeth and waited.

When we finally got going, the drive down itself was easy and speedy; Jane and I stopped the first night south of Lyons in France, then crossed the Alps via the Frejus tunnel. The delay cut down my recce time drastically, but I think I'll cope. I'll have to, because the house is let to someone else after our week, so there's no possibility of extending our stay.

JULY

The first day's shoot over, and already I'm slightly behind schedule. I had to take some time out today to talk to the owner of the house, Nicholas, a very pleasant and pukka Englishman who lives in a self-contained apartment at the side of the house.

For some reason he'd got it into his head that we were all here on assignment for *Vogue* magazine. Although he's been living in Italy for 20-odd years, I'm sure he's not so out of touch with English fashions that he imagines people back home are wandering around in the minimal garb my models are going to be clad in.

I don't know where on earth the confusion arose, because I explained in great detail the work I was going to be doing to Italian Chapters, the travel firm who organized the booking. But, rather than have any hiccups later on, I sat down with Nicholas over a drink and went through it all again, gently explaining that for quite a lot of the time the models weren't going to be wearing very much. Luckily, I had a couple of my previous calendars with me, and he was suitably complimentary when he leafed through them, so I think he's got the message that we're not shooting some blue movie epic in his beloved Borromei.

I can also see that I might have a little trouble with the outdoor shots, because the pool is a disappointment. It's pretty enough in itself, but the surrounding green hedgerow is rather bland and featureless. On the plus side, there's a long avenue of trees lined with classical statues leading away from the house. The sun coming through the foliage produces a pleasant dappled effect, and those statues provide exactly that strong sense of place I'm looking for.

****

Day two, and we're plugging on. The outdoor pictures are still proving awkward, because the weather is not as settled as I'd hoped. The significance of 'situated in the foothills of the Apuan Alps' didn't strike me when I read the brochure; mountain weather can be volatile, and the quick shifts are making pre-planning difficult. I'm setting up shots in brilliant sunshine, only to find that just as I've got everything in place, it has clouded over.

Nicholas is often pottering around the grounds while we're working, but he's perfectly affable, and doesn't get in the way.

Indoors, no problem. I'm almost spoilt for choice. I'm aiming for a mix of bedroom scenarios and around-the-house pictures with each girl, and I've already identified more settings than I need.

One or two will need careful handling, because the 'faded' is as true as the 'elegance' in some areas; for instance, the sitting room contains a beautiful eighteenth-century sofa, but I had to choose my angles carefully when shooting with Angela this afternoon, to avoid showing the sacking sagging out of the bottom of the frame.

Still, you can't build sets like this in a studio. One of the girls reminded me of that when we were shooting in my favourite bedroom of the five. Looking at the fresco-covered walls, she said: 'Must have cost thousands, that lot.' Not quite the reaction of an art connoisseur, but I know what she meant.

Changes of styling, lighting and location create three distinctly different looks using the same model

JULY

The end of the third day, and I'm almost back on schedule again. Location shooting always reminds me of the saying: 'If a man knows he's going to be hanged in a fortnight, it concentrates his mind wonderfully.' A strict deadline like the one I've got here certainly concentrates my mind, because the consequences of failure are too awful to contemplate.

Today was very productive, though – the sun shone, and I got a lot done outside. Partly, I made my own luck, I have to say. I'd been worrying I hadn't got enough outdoor locations, so I got up at the crack of dawn and went for a wander through the grounds. They're quite extensive, around 25 acres, and my late arrival meant that there were still areas I hadn't had a chance to explore.

Down towards the edge of the estate I stumbled across an olive grove which was being harvested. The fine-mesh nets that are spread on the ground to collect the olives were lying in shimmering bundles, looking for all the world like fairy gossamer, and the slightly surrealistic scene immediately suggested itself as a perfect location for later in the day.

90

Deciding what to include and what to leave out of a shot is largely a question of intuition – experience has a part to play, but mainly it's a question of making an imaginative leap, seeing objects and models in a different light.

If you gave 10 photographers the same model plus a shedful of assorted props, and told them they could use as many or as few of the shed's contents as they liked, you would get 10 radically different pictures. The concept of what makes a 'good' photograph is a very subjective one, except on the most basic level of technical competence, so what we're really talking about here is creativity. I like to think that one of the reasons clients choose me as opposed to any other photographer for a job is not just that I get the work done on time and within budget, important though that is, but that I have a way of looking at things that they appreciate.

****

'Why do you always drive at a hundred miles an hour, Jane?'

'Because you do, Geoff.'

I can't argue with that. We're zipping along the French autoroute heading for Calais. We're tired, frustrated after getting snarled up with the Paris Air Show traffic as we came round the Peripherique, Paris's answer to the M25, and eager to get home.

At least we haven't got hangovers today, though, which is more than anyone of us could have claimed yesterday as I left Borromei to drop everybody else off at the airport. Or rather, try to drop everybody else off at the airport, because we hadn't managed to get Helen, the last model we'd booked for the trip, a return ticket. I remember thinking at the time, it won't be a problem, there's always somebody who doesn't turn up for a flight. Wrong! So Helen is snoozing in the back seat.

The final day of any trip is always a struggle. There's equipment to pack up, tidying to be done, inventories to check, farewells to be made, planes to catch. And usually aspirins to take, because the relief of completing the assignment tends to have manifested itself in a general letting off of steam on the last night, a process often involving large quantities of food and drink.

Deep shadows, dark furniture and the splendour of the frescoes combine to create an air of sombre sensuality

JULY

We normally eat well on trips, it's a way of rewarding everyone after a hard day's work. At Borromei, we were delighted to discover a family-run restaurant right next to the house. The proprietors were equally delighted when we all descended on them the first night, and their cooking rose to the occasion.

Models can be finicky souls when it come to eating, which is understandable, because to a large extent their figures are their fortune, but it has driven me to distraction at times: 'Oh, I only eat steak and chips'; 'I can't stand fish'; 'Haven't they got any low-calorie salad cream?' I've heard them all in my time. I'm glad to say that on this trip the fussy-eater factor was minimal.

The highlight of the trip on the food front was undoubtedly the meal we had on that last night. Nicholas had recommended 'rather a nice little place' in Lucca, the nearest town to Borromei. What he hadn't told us was quite how plush it was. When we got into town we followed his directions, and found ourselves in front of an incredibly grand establishment set into the old wall of the town. It was a balmy summer's eve, and all the tables were set out on the grassy top of the wall.

I looked at the menu and gulped, because the prices matched the setting in extravagance, but fortunately Chris – who as the client was going to be footing the bill – is a chap of impeccable taste and a great lover of Italian food. I looked at him questioningly, he gave me the nod, and in we went for an exquisite evening. The ambience, the service, and not least the complimentary champagne to start with and liqueurs to finish, all made for a memorable evening. Definitely the treat of the trip.

It might have been wise to have left a little earlier than we did, but one liqueur led to another, then another ... and ultimately to that unpleasant sensation when you wake up the next

morning and find that your mouth is as dry as the Kalahari Desert, and for some reason your tongue seems to have stuck to the roof of your mouth. The models' idea of a practical joke didn't help matters, either – I nursed myself into the shower and started shampooing my hair, and couldn't understand why it seemed to be getting stickier rather than cleaner. I dolloped more shampoo on, but that only seemed to make matters worse. The little man practising his drums in my head didn't help, either.

I gave up trying to make sense of what was happening and stumbled out of the shower to brush my teeth. It may be your idea of fun to coat somebody's toothbrush with salt, but it certainly isn't mine. I never did find out if the perpetrator was the same person who'd emptied out my shampoo bottle and filled it with baby oil.

******

The deal is done. I'm shooting my last picture on my last day in Bond Street. Tomorrow I move to W12.

My last studio shoot in Bond Street, of Laura (bottom right), was a conscious attempt to match the mood of the Tuscany picture of Nikki (above right), as I was one photograph short for a calendar package of one-off shots

Events have moved at an astonishing speed since I came back from Tuscany. On my first day back in the studio my former agent, Denise, popped in for a chat. Although we came to an amicable parting of the ways from a business point of view, Denise had kept her office at the studio – I had the space, so there seemed absolutely no reason why not.

Denise told me that Gareth, one of the photographers in her existing stable, was looking for a new studio as the lease on his current premises, not far up the road, was expiring shortly. I know Gareth and get on with him well, and I realized that my studio would be ideal for him. He specializes in advertising still-life work, and often has several sets on the go at the same time, so needs a fair amount of space. And having his agent actually on the premises would be a bonus.

Gareth and I had a drink that evening, and did the deal more or less on the spot. We agreed what we both regarded as a reasonable price for the lease and the fixtures and fittings – I left most of the furniture behind, plus all the flats and set-building materials and my Colorama backdrops. The only thing that slightly pained me was that I'd just installed a new kitchen at some expense, but you can't win 'em all.

I'm feeling in good shape, though. I thought I might be rather depressed when I left Bond Street. Sixteen years is a long time, after all. Somewhat to my surprise, my overwhelming emotion was one of relief. I don't think I'd realized quite how much the financial burden of keeping the old studio running was getting to me. Jane says she's noticed a great improvement in my state of mind – I'm obviously being too nice to her.

Now I've got a different burden, one of time, not money. I'm scrambling to get my new place organized and at the same time trying to crack on with my last big calendar of the year for Moments, a studio-based production entitled *Reflections*. I want to get it out of the way well before the end of the month, because I want to grab a holiday with the family. And I'm planning another working trip in early September, to Portugal this time, to keep that slave driver Dave Muscroft topped up with material.

Although I was fairly ruthless about what I needed to bring with me from Bond Street, there is no way everything is going to fit into the existing storage space I've inherited in West London. So, I'm having my office fitted out with more shelving, plus a light-box to view the transparencies when I'm editing.

This pose accentuates Sandra's long slim legs, while a little snoot of light prevents her face from merging into the blue surround

AUGUST

Amid the crashing and banging, I'm trying to concentrate my mind on *Reflections*. In one sense, the job is similar to Tuscany: four models, four days of solid shooting. But what to shoot, that's the question.

The way forward now is to make a decision on the propping, do a test session to experiment with the lighting, and let Moments see some Polaroids of the results. I've had one idea for props that I want to try out – I went round to dinner with a film cameraman friend of mine the other evening, and the walls of his dining room are lined with clapperboards from the productions he's worked on. Using accessories with a film theme – clapperboards, cameras, film-set chairs with names stencilled on the back – would give the calendar a link running through all twelve pictures. I'll play around with the idea and use something along these lines in the test. I don't want to start this job until I'm absolutely sure that everyone – not least me – is happy we're on the right track.

****

Steve and the rest of the Moments crowd love the tests. They like them rather more than I do, in fact. I still don't think I've got the lighting right, but I do think I know how I can improve it. And I've made the props decision. Pursuing my film idea, I went to a props company which had all the paraphernalia I'd been thinking of, but when they dug everything out and dumped it in front of me on the warehouse floor, I started having second thoughts. The theme began to feel rather contrived.

One item did grab my attention, though: an industrial fan. These are used as wind machines by film-makers, and this one was a tiddler in comparison to the heavy-duty models used to simulate storms or to blow Marilyn Monroe's skirt up around her hips in ... in ... whatever movie it was where she had her skirt blown up around her hips. The model I was looking at was the size used for the windswept hair look, and when I tried it in the test session, the combination of billowing hair and the giant shadows the model projected against the backdrop convinced me I was heading in the right direction, even if I hadn't quite got there yet.

Because shadows are the feature I'm going to major on, I think – apart from the girls, of course. Having decided that, and junked the film-set concept, I've assembled a collection of mod-ernistic wrought-iron furniture, which chimes in well with the fan in style. I hope.

****

I'm not sorry to have got rid of those props. It's all very well moving to a smaller studio, but I've paid a high price in barked shins this week. That apart, the *Reflections* shoot exceeded my hopes.

It was one of those jobs that seemed to take on a life of its own, as new ideas occurred to me while I was in the middle of shooting. It may not sound as if I had a big task on my hands compared to my workload in Tuscany, because I was shooting far fewer frames. At Borromei I was working in at least three different locations each day, indoors and out, and shooting variations of pose, angle and styling in each. Here I only had to produce three individual shots each day for four days.

I say 'only', but each shot had to be exactly right. I had absolutely no margin for error, because each model was hired for the day, and to go back and do a reshoot of any one day would have entailed an unacceptably high overrun on the budget. (When we were planning the job, I'd asked Moments for six days to shoot the job in, but the budget wouldn't stretch that far.)

For each shot I had to move the furniture out of the set, move the new props in, relight the set, and then do a Polaroid test of the new set-up. Meanwhile, the model had to have a complete change of make-up and outfit.

Of all these factors, the lighting gave me the most trouble at the outset. For the original test, I'd rigged up the lighting to give me direct flash, then added a spotlight on the girl, giving me the background shadows I was looking for. It worked well enough, but it was rather obvious; somehow it lacked spark. When I came to shoot the first picture, I was resigned to using that lighting set-up, because I had to start pressing the button at that point or risk falling behind the clock.

AUGUST

Everything was in place, and as I looked through the viewfinder and shot the first frame the answer literally came to me in a flash. As the lights fired and I saw the shadows for a split second, I saw the solution – instead of throwing shadows of the models on to the background, I should be throwing shadows of the props.

I fired off a few more frames with the existing lighting, more out of habit than anything else, then stopped and rearranged the lights. I focused the spot on the fan rather than the model, and added an extra little spot, a snoot to narrow the light beam down, to pick out one little detail of the model's body. I did another Polaroid to check the results and bingo! The result was a thousand times better.

That gave me the confidence to carry on experimenting throughout the rest of the shots, and the job turned into one of those happy experiences where I was working at full creative stretch, and enjoying myself at the same time. I made the make-up punchier, and tinkered with the lighting again, adjusting the density of the soft blue gel I was washing over the whole set. Then the fan and the gel started me thinking of those hot, steamy nights we've all seen featured in American movies, where the heroine tries to cool herself down in a heatwave as the neon signs from the bar across the road wink on and off.

And what do people do when there's a heatwave? They sweat. So I started introducing some water into the equation. I shot every set-up dry at first, then introduced a little bit of moisture. After that, I sprayed the model more comprehensively, and for the final frames of each scenario I went right over the top, drenching the poor girls by the bucketful.

When I came to edit the transparencies, this variety helped me give the final selection a progression, a pace, that it would otherwise have lacked. The final results were radically different from the original concept, but I ended the four days absolutely sure in my own mind that they were just about the best work I could have done within the framework of the brief. There's actually very little nudity, but I find that calendar very erotic, very mysterious.

****

AUGUST

My golf isn't getting any better. I joined the family down in Cornwall for a week's holiday after I'd finished *Reflections*, and my son, Eddie, gave me a beating on the local courses. While I'm pleased he's playing well, it doesn't do the ego good to lose to a 14-year-old.

I'm back at the studio now, licking my wounds, catching up with my admin and planning to get in some sneaky practice when I go off to the Algarve with Ralph for a week of magazine and library stock shooting next month.

My American agent is coming over in a couple of days, so I'm sorting out some material for him to take back for the US market.

This set of pictures should suit him. They're a couple of years old now, but have sold so well elsewhere that I've only just got them back from Dave Muscroft. I can't even remember the name of the model now – all I can remember is that she was English, but had lived in Australia for a number of years.

What I do know is that it was the only job she ever did in England. She'd been modelling in Australia and came back to England toying with the idea of settling over here again. She signed up with a model agency and did this shoot for me, then decided to return to Oz.

I shot down in Kent, in a cornfield by this old thatched cottage owned by a former model who'd kept in touch with me after she married and retired to a life of rural domesticity. I'd intended to shoot an indoor set, because I never trust the English weather, but that day the sun was gorgeous – a golden afternoon light – so I changed my mind.

****

A flexible attitude is important on any shoot. I hadn't originally planned to work outdoors on this English country house shoot, but when the sun came out I took advantage of the beautiful light

AUGUST

And I might as well have another go at trying to flog this beach set of a model named Michele, which I shot on spec during an earlier Portuguese trip, because Dave's returned it for a more negative reason – he can't shift it anywhere. For the life of me I can't understand why. I'm quite fond of it. Every picture tells a story, but I don't like this one. Perhaps the Americans will provide a happy ending.

Sand acts as a natural reflector on the beach, providing fill-in lighting. Michele's headband enhances the desired 'back to nature' look

Ralph and I are developing into a bit of a mutual admiration society. We got on well enough when we first met in Kos, but it's only since we've been working out of the same studio that we've realized quite how closely our views on the work we do coincide.

We're both quite straight compared to some of the rip-off artists in the business; we respect our models, for instance, which is regarded as slightly quaint and old-fashioned in some quarters. But we like to treat the girls that work for us properly, both in a personal and a financial sense, even if occasionally it hurts our pockets.

For instance, I was offered a great deal of money by a British magazine some while ago for some pictures I'd taken of a girl called Kim Mills, who went on to appear in a James Bond movie. My problem was that when I photographed her it was on the strict understanding that the resulting pictures were to be sold in overseas markets only.

I do a fair amount of work for the magazine concerned, and they brought a great deal of pressure to bear on me to release the pictures. When I said I didn't have the rights to sell the pictures in Britain they said not to worry, they'd sort out the legal side of things, and when I still wouldn't play they upped their offer several times.

Maybe they thought I was playing hard to get, trying to be cute and holding out for a higher price. But no amount of money would have induced me to part with those pictures. I've got a reputation for being fair and honest, and I want to keep it.

****

Ralph takes the same view, on that and most other aspects of our work, which makes for an easy atmosphere around the place and is a great relief to me, because it's always a bit of a leap into the unknown when you first start working alongside someone so closely. During my years in Bond Street I rented space to a number of other photographers, and while I got on well enough with most of them, one or two of them had annoying little habits which drove me to distraction.

A still-life photographer called Fred, for instance, was one of the pleasantest people I've ever met. As part of the deal we'd struck when he came in, he shared some of my studio equipment, and he would never put anything back in its proper place, instead just dumping it on the nearest flat surface. Many of the items he photographed would arrive in cartons, and as each successive load came in he'd pile up the empty boxes against the wall and leave them there.

As the months went by, the area he was left to shoot in grew smaller and smaller, because the wall of cartons began to close in on him. And when I walked through his steadily shrinking floor space there was a constant scrunch as I trod on the empty film boxes and wrappings that littered the floor. I couldn't work like that, and after a while I decided he couldn't either, at least not in my studio.

With Ralph, no problem. And once I've got out of my annoying habit of playing the radio too loud when I'm working, I think he'll agree that he has no problem with me.

****

Getting together our Algarve trip was a scramble, as one model dropped out at the last minute and we had to rush round and find a replacement. It's all very well nice guys like us showing respect, but I have to say that not all models seem duly grateful.

The early-evening sun coming over Justine's shoulder gives her hair a striking rim light. Added light is reflected from a wall just out of shot, and the very short depth of field pushes the flowers in the background and foreground out of focus, centring attention where it is wanted

SEPTEMBER

Now we've all arrived – Ralph and Emma, the make-up artist we've brought in place of Claire, who's not available this time, had to come out on a later flight than the rest of us in the end, because bookings are very heavy this year – the first thing Ralph and I have to do is to mark out our territory. That may make us sound like wild animals in some natural history programme, but in fact it's just common sense. We've brought three models out with us, plus Emma, who also models and is keen to earn some extra loot by working in front of the camera as well as behind the scenes. If I can fit her into the schedule, why not? So, Ralph and I will each be shooting the same girls, and while we have different styles it would be daft for us to use the same locations as well.

The key to an operation like this is to make sure that where you're staying gives you enough options. There's no point in renting some pokey little villa with a pocket-handkerchief garden, because you'll run out of locations in no time flat. You need space, and privacy. I take a great deal of care selecting the places I book for trips. I ask the villa companies, and the villa owners if necessary, for additional information if I'm unsure of a place, and generally make a nuisance of myself until I'm absolutely convinced everything is right, because once I've arrived there's no turning back ... well, I suppose there is, but not without wasting a great deal of money.

This villa is nothing out of the ordinary, certainly not in the same class as Borromei, but it's more than adequate. Five bedrooms, a pool, a garden that slopes down to a lake, a verandah and two patios, and complete privacy. Time to unleash the camera and get cracking.

****

The first thing I nearly cracked was someone's head. Here we are, having come all this way to get some decent light, and the first outdoor session I set up lasts about two minutes. The model can't work in the sunlight. The minute she took her dark glasses off she started squinting, and her eyes began to water. It looks to me like she's got conjunctivitis.

It may not be her fault. She swears she didn't know she had a problem until we started working. But I have my suspicions. Ralph and I are only going to be able to use her indoors, which rather defeats the object of bringing her out here in the first place. And it's doubly annoying because I'd intended to use her for a bonus job I'd picked up just before we left.

The swimwear shoot that was cancelled earlier in the year is still a painful memory. But my previous work for the company has paid dividends, because four days before we left for Portugal one of their former executives, John, phoned me up to suggest a drink. We'd always got on well, and the drink turned into lunch. As we chatted, he told me he was now working for a rival swimwear outfit, and needed some catalogue shots in a hurry.

He didn't have a very big budget, certainly not one enough to cover the costs of a full-scale trip, but then he didn't need that many pictures, either. When I told him I was shortly off to Portugal, everything slotted into place. We went back to the studio, he looked at the models and the location, and felt confident they would fit the bill. A couple of phone calls later and he was booked to come out to Portugal for three days, during which I'd do a day-and-a-half's work for him.

This meant that I was shooting slightly less speculative work than I'd planned, but the beauty of this job for John is that it suits both parties down to the ground. I've got a firm commission for a very fair fee, and he's going to get his pictures at a fraction of the cost of funding an entire trip. But it's only going to work if the models can work in and around the pool. You don't see too many swimwear catalogues which have been photographed indoors ...

****

John's arrived, and fortunately he thinks we can get away without using Miss Pink Eyes. That's cheered me up, because I've got a second model problem. One of the girls has decided she doesn't want to do any magazine work. I could make her, because that was definitely the agreement with her agency before we came, but there's no point – if a model is bored or unhappy with what she's doing, it shows in the pictures, believe me. This trip has got more than its fair share of model aggravation. I can see I'm not going to get anywhere near a golf course.

****

My last afternoon, and Emma and I are literally chasing the light round the villa as the sun drops. She's been pestering me to take some pictures of her ever since we got here; I did try early one evening, but it clouded over before we got going. I haven't got much time left this time, either, so I'm not attempting to build up a full magazine set of pictures; just going for individual shots. Emma's working well, I must say – no problem with boredom here – but I'm beginning to flag because I started work very early this morning, doing a session with Miss Pink Eyes.

Shot in rapidly fading light, the starkness of these pictures is accentuated by the shadows and black-and-white background, with Emma's flesh tones and lipstick the only points of colour

SEPTEMBER

My bedroom faces due East, and the first morning after we arrived I woke up to see the early-morning sun just breaking through the branches of the trees, throwing some very moody patterns on to the back wall of my room. I made a mental note then to use that light, but hadn't managed to fit it into the schedule before.

Not for the first time on this trip, things didn't work out quite as planned. We were up before dawn, Emma did a great natural-make-up job, the model was looking great ... and then the sun refused to come out. I sat there gazing furiously at the grey sky and thought, I'm all set up, I've got to get something out of this. We'd brought a minimal amount of lighting equipment with us, so I rushed round and set up the lights, trying to get as close to a natural daylight effect as possible, but knowing that I wasn't going to have the patterns created by the branches that had been the reason for shooting in this location in the first place.

When I did a Polaroid test, though, I cheered up, because it looked very very good. My theme for the set was a reverse striptease, with the model getting out of bed, then slowly getting dressed, and it worked like a charm. (Although I was amused when the set was published, because the magazine which bought it reverted to a formal striptease sequence, starting off with the fully-clothed shots. So much for my attempt to give them something different.)

****

The final joke in our Portuguese comedy of errors was on Ralph. He and Emma were due to leave 12 hours after us, and Ralph had planned a solid day's shooting. But the pair of them had only been working for half-an-hour or so before the local agent rolled up with the next tenants, demanding the villa be vacated immediately. Bit of a confusion about times...

The curious thing is that after all the annoyances on the trip, all the pictures have turned out brilliantly, and are selling very well. And it's given us some tales to tell.

Jane says it's our fault for not inviting her to Portugal. She's come over today to assist me on an advertising shoot, because although she's steadily establishing herself as a photographer, she still gets the occasional quiet period, and this is one of them. For my part, I value her help, advice, and – possibly most important of all – her sense of humour.

When I left Bond Street, Jane felt it was a natural time to go it alone and concentrate on getting her own work while doing a little freelance assisting on the side, rather than the other way round, as it had been when she worked for me full-time. She's still based in the same building as my former studio, having taken a small office on another floor. When she needs studio space she either rents my old place from Gareth or, if that's not free, a studio on the floor below belonging to another photographer. She's starting to get busier, and we're both keeping our fingers crosssed behind our backs that she'll soon get her first really big job – she's pitched for a national poster and advertising campaign for Ruddles Beer, and the talks are going well.

OCTOBER

An in-and-out month. As fast as the money comes in, Ralph and I are paying it out again on new lighting equipment. We've decided to pool our resources in this area, as we've become rather fed up with continually creating lighting set-ups in the studio, only to have to dismantle everything to take with us when we go on location. And juggling dates has proved a bit of a pain – we've had problems if one of us wanted to shoot in the studio on the same day as the other was off on location.

Basically, we just didn't have enough equipment, hence the spending spree. To be honest, Ralph's bank balance is bearing the brunt – we've agreed that I put my Bowens quads, which are quite bulky but powerful and ideal for the studio, into the kitty, while Ralph has bought a Bowens Traveller kit, which is more compact and suited to location work, as his part of the deal. And, between us, we've also added to our stock of accessories: spots, small snoots, Fresnel snoots, honeycomb snoots, all designed to create different effects. So from now on, we can leave the studio fully rigged all the time.

There's a certain bedding-down period with any new equipment. It takes a while to get used to it. A central difference is in the colour balance. After working with the same set of lights for a while, you become accustomed to the particular quality of light it provides. With a new set, you have to go through the learning process all over again.

Shooting with the Bowens Traveller outfit and a couple of my original softboxes, I've found that the effect isn't as warm as with my quads, so I've had to change my colour-correcting filters – for the technically minded, I've switched from a colder 10 Blue filter to a 5 Blue, in order to tone down the warming effect produced by the Fuji film and my colour laboratory combined. Yet Ralph, shooting on Kodachrome, has discovered through trial and error that he needs to add more warmth, by means of a yellow 81A filter, to achieve the same flesh tones.

There are no short cuts to this process – we're having to plug away until we're so familar with the lighting we could shoot blindfold ... on second thoughts, that's not a very clever comparison, but you know what I mean, and there is no way of comparing

flesh tones without having some flesh to start with, so we've set up the Bowens Traveller in the studio and are busily working our way through test shots of potential models before risking it on a money job.

It's not a total chore, though, because I enjoy experimenting with lighting, filtration and exposures, and playing around with over-exposing and under-processing film to see what effects this produces. I'm still learning, still enjoying taking pictures most of the time.

But when I discover a new technique, stumble on a different approach, my first instinct is to wonder whether it has a commercial application,because I'm not a great believer in photography as an art form. I find a lot of exhibitions of photographs meaningless, because the pictures are so often divorced from their proper context.

OCTOBER

There are very few of my photographs that I would want to see framed and hanging on a wall, because that's not what I took them for. If I shoot a session for a magazine, I like to see the end result laid out on the printed page, type and all. If I take a picture for a poster, I want to see it on a billboard, because I've shot it with that presentation in mind. Up there it has an impact that would be destroyed if it were reduced and framed.

Take the set of Sophie I've just shot, my first with the new lights. I know that the magazine editor I'm aiming them at wants a choice of horizontal and vertical poses, and prefers a fairly tight crop on the model, without too fussy a background. So that's what I give him. While I add an element of creativity in my choice of pose, styling and location, I do so firmly in a commercial framework.

The calendar side of my work probably gives me more scope for originality, because calendars are produced to less of a formula than men's magazines, and the brief is less rigid.

As I've said before, deciding what photographs to take is often harder than actually taking them. That's why it's good to have such a close rapport with the Moments crowd. I've mentioned the hassles I've endured with indecisive clients in the past, but the flip side of the coin – a client who insists on sticking to a totally unworkable concept – can be equally frustrating.

A few years ago, I had a calendar commission for a spare parts manufacturer who had fixed firmly on an idea before talking to me. They were trying to emphasize that their product range was international, that they supplied bits not only for British cars, but also for Japanese cars, French cars, German cars, and so on. They also wanted to get over that they offered an efficient, friendly service.

So far, so good. The trouble was that the marketing man in charge of the operation had delusions of creative grandeur. He was – how shall I put it kindly – of a slightly older generation to mine. His idea of an erotic picture was a model wearing a French maid outfit, all short skirt and suspender tops, pouting pertly to camera. And it got worse – the overworked image he'd come up with was of a girl in that get-up delivering breakfast on a tray (service, get it?) which consisted of coffee, croissants and a copy of *Le Monde* (international, get it?) to a grinning mechanic working on a French car.

The brief was so top-heavy with concept it lost all coherence as a photographic image, and their maintenance garage that they wanted me to use as a set wasn't any better: my heart sank when I walked into this vast barn of a place to see piles of tyres, white-painted walls, a row of work benches and not a lot else. It had no atmosphere at all.

I argued it out with them, but I couldn't budge them from the French maid folly. So I had a choice of either turning down the commission, or trying somehow to rescue it.

It crossed my mind more than once to tell them to find another photographer, but the thought of all those bills stacking up on my desk shut my mouth. I went away and thought about it, and came to the conclusion that I had a chance of salvaging the shoot if I changed the set.

My idea was to create a stylized garage, one with some character. I used the garage in the film of Roald Dahl's *Danny the Champion of the World* as a mental reference, and built a complete set with a late forties, early fifties air to it within the company's garage. Advertising signs and plenty of cans, all of the right period, tongue-and-groove pine for the walls, and a fake window so I could get some depth and inject artificial daylight. I even commandeered a caravan to use as a changing room. And the company was very happy with the end result, which on some jobs is the best you can say.

****

Sophie's outrageously expensive Lycra outfit, courtesy of a generous PR company, establishes a mood of casual luxury which emphasizes her femininity

OCTOBER

I was glad to see that I wasn't alone in having problems like these when I watched a TV documentary about David Bailey and his struggles to shoot a calendar for Unipart, another car parts manufacturer – what is it with them? – during the Le Mans 24-hour race. The idea of using the event as a backdrop for the models was logical enough, but in practice it soon became obvious that it was a logistical nightmare.

Relying on a once-a-year happening to provide the atmosphere for the pictures was always going to be tough, because the race organizers and teams had other priorities than putting themselves out just to please Bailey, big name though he is. He was faced with too many random factors for comfort, he wasn't in control of his location, and short of having a full-scale dummy run 12 months beforehand, there was no way he was ever going to be.

What was interesting for me was to see how Bailey coped with the problems. He had two choices: muddle along with the original concept, with a bit of tinkering here and there, and hope it would be all right on the night; or start again from scratch.

Bailey didn't disappoint me. He said long and strong that the idea was a bum one, and then sat down and dreamt up an entirely new concept, which did work. He obviously still cares after all these years. And so do I.

******

OCTOBER

I decided on a sentimental journey for my second try-out with the new lights, and called up my old friend Virginia. She owns the antique shop where I photographed the first set of pictures I ever sold, but when I moved to Bond Street I lost touch with her. Years later, I was looking through a directory of locations and there her name was, accompanying pictures of a house stocked with, you've guessed it, antiques.

I knew the area well, so got in touch, and she kindly offered me a mate's rate rather than charging me her full fee. I use the house several times a year, as much out of pleasure at seeing Virginia again as anything else. I feel comfortable there, and there is certainly no shortage of props.

****

Jane's just completed the Ruddles job, and they love it. Whoopee! This is the big one she's been waiting for.

What made us both laugh was that she's discovered she only got the career-changing opportunity to do the Ruddles shoot by mistake. The agency that gave her the commission called her in again the week after she'd successfully completed it to discuss another still-life commission. Off she went with her portfolio, which is full of people and fashion pictures, and the creative director leafed through it, looking more and more puzzled, then said: 'Where's all your still-life stuff?'

'Er ... I haven't got any,' replied Jane. 'Except for the Ruddles job I've just done for you.'

'I could have sworn you were a still-life photographer,' the adman said. 'Where's the portfolio I saw before I gave you Ruddles?'

'This is the portfolio you saw,' Jane said firmly. And, because she'd done good work for Ruddles, they gave her the job.

Whatever the inhabitants may claim, America isn't the land of the free – everything costs. The good news is that most things don't cost much more than they do in Britain, at least as far as photography is concerned. Models, locations, and equipment hire won't break the bank.

Of course, there is always the little matter of the air fare. While I've worked in America on a number of occasions, it's always

been on commission, so someone else has picked up the tab. It never occurred to me it would be an economic proposition to go and shoot speculative material over there, but my American agent, Ben, has persuaded me that it's not such a daft idea.

He's going to be out in Los Angeles later this month, and he's suggested I go out and join him. He says it would be good public relations for me to meet

some of my American clients, and he also says that even at this time of year I've got a reasonable chance of weather good enough for shooting outdoors.

Neither of those arguments really convinces me, I must say – as far as meeting the people who buy my work over there is concerned, I honestly don't think it makes a great deal of difference. They're not going to commission me to shoot for them in England, and if they like the stuff I'm already syndicating to them via Ben, which they do, then presumably they'll carry on buying it whether I meet them or not.

But Ben has made one point I find persuasive. He says the model scene in California is definitely a buyer's market, and that I'll be spoilt for choice. There's a definite shortage of new talent at home at the moment, so the thought of all those tanned valley girls hungry for work has made me sit up and take notice.

I can only spare about eight days away from London this month, because I'm heavily into some commissioned fashion work, but I'm tempted. Even if I don't make a profit on this trip, with luck I'll make enough contacts to be able to return for more cost-effective trips in the future.

Stephanie arrived for our booking in this glitzy outfit. It reminded me of a Wild West saloon girl, so I pursued that theme while shooting

One thing I don't bless the country for is Thanksgiving Day, though. I could brain Ben for suggesting this particular week for me to come out, because I've discovered that Thanksgiving is like a Bank Holiday – many places are closed, as people have the family round for a big lunch, turkey and all the trimmmings, to celebrate ... well, I'm not quite sure what they are celebrating, except that it's got something to do with that bunch of Pilgrim Fathers who sailed over from Plymouth in sixteen hundred and whatever. I haven't got anything to celebrate though, because it means a precious day lost from an already tight schedule.

In fairness, though, Ben has been a great deal of help. He knows which girls have already been shot for the UK market, and are therefore girls I won't want to use, and he's taken me round to the model agencies he reckons are the most promising around at the moment.

The usual jobsworth attitude from the security staff at Heathrow. I don't know why I bother to have the argument these days, but I just think it's an admission of failure if I don't even try to get my film hand-checked rather than put through an X-ray scanner.

The conversation follows a well-worn path. I ask for a hand check, and it's refused. I ask why, and the answer is: 'It's against policy.' I'm then told that the level of radiation is so low that it can't possibly damage the film. I reply that one dose of radiation may not cause any problems, but that repeated doses might well do, as the radiation builds up each time. Quite often on trips I'm going through a number of airports. For example, the last time I went to LA I was on my way to Arizona for a fashion shoot, and my flying itinerary was London-LA, LA-Phoenix, then Phoenix-Tuscon, followed on my return trip by Tuscon-LA, LA-Monterey, back to LA, and finally home to London.

Fortunately, in the States they still have the quaint notion that the customer is often right. 'Hand check, sir? Certainly.' God bless America.

****

NOVEMBER

Booking models in the States is a very different, and in many ways a far more unsatisfactory, proposition than in England. Over in LA, the agencies show you their model books, and you have to make a booking from the photographs – the idea that you might want to meet the girls first, or do test shots, causes a great deal of confusion. Very rarely do you get a go-see before-hand.

I had a bizarre experience with the Playboy agency, an offshoot of the magazine operation. I knew of them because earlier in the year I'd asked them to send me their book; at the time, there was a possibility I might be asked to shoot a calendar in California. The book never arrived, the job never material-ized, but as I was now on the spot I phoned them up, said I was in town and wanted to come along to talk to them about models.

The receptionist was very polite, but said I couldn't come along without an appointment. I said, yes, that's why I'm phoning up, to make an appointment ... Ah, but you need an appoint-ment, came the reply. Is it me or is it them? I thought – one of us is

crazy, that's for sure. Finally I got put through to someone else, who explained that because of the *Playboy* name they got a number of sickos who use the freephone number listed in the Yellow Pages to make a free dirty phone call. A bit cheeky, I thought – even nutters should be prepared to pay for their pleasures.

On the plus side, the money aspect of booking models is very straightforward. You pay the agency a fee up front, about 10 per cent of the model fee, and then pay the girl her money on the day of shooting. It's a dead straight system, and while it doesn't help cash flow, it does avoid the complications that can sometimes arise in London, when you get an invoice from an agency some time after a shoot for a figure which bears little relation-ship to what you thought you'd agreed.

Although winter days are short, on the plus side the light never gets high enough to create those awkward summer noonday shadows. In LA it was warm enough to photograph April out of doors in November

The models are different, too. In most cases, they're far more brash and up-front than their European counterparts. They tend to be quite forceful, their attitude seems to be, I'm a professional, I know what I'm doing, so you just snap away and I'll choose the poses. Maybe it's the Hollywood influence – just about every model you meet in LA is there because she wants to get into the film business. However professional her attitude is to modelling she views it as a stepping-stone to stardom rather than as a career in its own right. Most of them are going to be disappointed, of course, but that's showbusiness.

Perhaps because they have to be pushy if they want to get anywhere in films, this attitude carries over into their modelling. They tend to be less subtle – what you see is what you get.

And quite a lot of it is silicone. Americans of both sexes seem to have an obsession about breasts. The men like big ones, and many women seem to think they're failures if they can't provide. So they trot off to the nearest plastic surgeon and get 'em fixed. The first model I photographed in LA, Stephanie, cheerfully owned up to her silicone implants, liposuction operation to give her bee-sting lips, and hair extensions – her attitude was: 'If I don't think I can make myself look good enough, I know a man who can'.

She was fun to work with, though, I have to say, because she didn't take herself too seriously. Life seemed to be one big joke as far as she was concerned, although she was a hard worker. Apart from modelling, she was big on the go-go dancing circuit, and calculated she earned about $5,000 a week. Judging by her expensive outfit, and the brand-new Corvette she rolled up in, most of those earnings didn't hang about in her bank account too long.

I photographed her at a house in Hollywood, situated in a road just off Laurel Canyon Drive, which is reputed to have the highest suicide rate in America. Apparently it's a favoured spot for suicidees to come and drive their cars down the ravine, and if it's a slow month for drive-in death, the film industry types and their families who live in the road's plush houses do their best to keep up the average by taking overdoses.

The owner of the house, Ron, had been in the film business himself, albeit on the accountancy side, before he wisely retired early. It had a hauntingly familiar air, and I found out later that practically every English photographer who visits LA is introduced to Ron and his house, so I had probably seen it in some one else's pictures. But it suited me, it was an excellent location.

Despite what Ben said, the weather wasn't that brilliant while I was out there. I arrived at night and booked into a hotel on Sunset Strip, and when I got up the next morning and opened the curtains I was greeted by a clear blue sky, absolutely brilliant light for shooting. I spent two days rushing around in the sunshine organizing myself, and of course by the third day, my first day for shooting, the LA smog had descended, and a haze sat over the entire city. To cover myself, I hired some lighting equipment, because although I wanted to shoot Stephanie by Ron's pool, I had to make sure I got something; and we did indeed end up shooting indoors.

While Stephanie was fun, my favourite model of the four I ended up shooting on the trip was April, who wasn't American at all, but a half-Cherokee Indian Canadian, and wasn't even a professional model. After all my rushing around making appointments with agencies, I found her completely by chance. I walked past a shopfront with a sign hanging outside saying 'Model Agency', and popped in on the off-chance.

I explained I was from England and what I was looking for, and the initial response was distinctly discouraging. This agency wasn't really into photographic models at all, they majored in advertising, promotional and publicity work. Their girls spent most of their time doing live appearances to tout the virtues of various products in supermarkets and at exhibitions.

The young guy running the place said he'd see what he could do, but didn't hold out much hope of finding anyone suitable. I gave him my hotel address, but left thinking he was just going through the motions out of politeness, and I didn't expect to hear from him again.

I'm glad to say I was wrong though, because he got in touch the next morning, and when I went down to see him again he produced pictures of half-a-dozen models, out of which April shone like a beacon.

One of the reasons I liked her was because she was different. She had those high Indian cheekbones, contrasted by piercing blue eyes, and although when I met her in the flesh I discovered her body wasn't perfect, few model's bodies are.

In April's case, she didn't at the time have the tautest of tums – the legacy of having recently given birth and then slimming down again – but it was nothing that couldn't be hidden. Water is often an ally when I want to disguise a blemish – if you can't crop it out or cover it up, slosh some water over it, is my motto.

The shoot was simplicity itself. Although she hadn't done much modelling, April was a natural, 'a good little worker', if that's not too patronizing. I posed her in front of a waterfall with minimal propping, just a bit of scarf, using a gold reflector to utilize the light coming from behind the waterfall as a fill and adjusting my exposure accordingly. The effect I was trying for, a bleached-out background contrasted with correct exposure for the face and body, worked perfectly.

****

Back home, I managed to sell enough material from the trip to almost break even, although that didn't account for my time as well.

DECEMBER

My favourite magazine set of the year arose from a casual conversation. Nikki, a model who I've known for a long time, popped into the studio for a purely social visit, her main aim being to show me the photographs of her recent wedding. And a romantic tale it was, too. Her boyfriend announced one day that he'd booked up a holiday in Barbados, and casually mentioned that he'd arranged for them to get married while they were out there. So she enjoyed a proposal, a holiday, a wedding and a honeymoon all in the space of a couple of weeks.

The marriage ceremony took place on the beach, but Nikki had taken out the full regalia with her to Barbados, and looked stunning, if a trifle incongruous, standing there in the sand and sunshine in a traditional wedding dress.

'You look sensational; I'd love to photograph you in that dress,' I said jokingly, but she immediately seized on the idea and replied: 'Why not? Why don't you put together a shoot?'

I didn't need to be asked twice. The set was very simple, a painted studio backdrop, and I focused the lighting on Nikki and her cream dress, letting the background fade into shadow. The pictures sold instantaneously.

Years ago, I regularly used to take pictures of models in wedding dresses for *Brides* magazine, but none of them were quite like these. The set of Nikki definitely had more the mood of the wedding night than the wedding day.

****

I'm definitely going to do only one more shoot before Christmas. I've decided I need a break. Like Norman Fowler, I'm going to spend more time with my family. And I have to prepare myself for the rigours of my birthday on New Year's Eve.

I also need a bit of thinking time. As I crash on through the year from one job to the next, I rarely get the opportunity to sit back and assess where I'm going in the long term.

To some extent that is out of my control as it depends on the market forces in operation. In the last couple of years I've shot more pictures for men's magazines than I did in the previous half-dozen years. While I enjoy the work, I think I've consolidated that area as much as I want to. I could do more, but I don't want to become a production-line photographer in the way that some people in the field are. They shoot exclusively for magazines, and bang out set after set featuring the same limited repertoire of stock poses. Sure, they make money, but in terms of creative stimulus they might as well be taking passport photographs.

Nikki's wedding dress has obvious erotic overtones. The choice of a painted backdrop rather than a realistic location was deliberate, to emphasize the fantasy nature of the session

DECEMBER

Some photographers have their own gimmicks, which I grant you can be successful enough in purely commercial terms. One I know of has taken the philosophy of specialization to new heights, or perhaps it should be widths. He pays for models to have breast-enlargement operations which boost their statistics to astonishingly inflated proportions. Before he comes across with the money for the operation, though, he signs the girl to an exclusive photographic contract for a minimum of a year, and then hawks the pictures around the more sensationalist, down-market publications that can't get enough of that type of stuff.

A variation I find more amusing is the latex scam. The art of special-effects make-up has reached new degrees of skill in recent years, and the creation of a pair of realistic-looking 60-inch Z-cup specials from soft rubber is all in a day's work for a practised operator. While it's not something I'm in a hurry to try myself – on a model, I mean – at least the girl doesn't have to carry around the zeppelins she's been endowed with, as they're strictly a one-day wonder.

So what do I want to try? Well, variety is the key word, I suppose. I also want to keep up my quota of trips, because they tend to charge my creative batteries. Each one is different, each presents a new set of circumstances to confront. And, with a few notable exceptions, they're fun.

There's a natural tendency in most of us to maximize the problems we face, to stress the difficult nature of our work in order to show ourselves in a better light when we reach a successful outcome. I catch myself doing this especially when talking about trips, although the truth is that I enjoy them practically without exception.

Looking back over what I've written about the previous months, I'm struck by the number of enjoyable moments I haven't mentioned. Take Kos, for instance – writing about that trip, I never mentioned the party that all the amateurs threw on our last night, a truly memorable barbecue that left its mark on most of us for a couple of days.

Nor did I mention, when talking about my LA trip, what happened when I went down to the coast, scouting for locations. I was up on the dunes early one morning on a near-deserted beach just past Malibu when two girls came along, left their clothes and bags in a pile, and went for a swim. Shortly afterwards, when the girls were well out to sea, two guys came down the beach and stopped by the pile.

Suddenly, one of them bent down and started rummaging in the bags, coming up with a camera in his hand. I tensed up, thinking I was watching a robbery in progress. They were rather large, the two of them, and I started having an inner debate; on the one hand, I would have felt a real wimp doing nothing, on the other hand, America has a reputation as a violent place, and it's not unusual for people to carry weapons ....

I'll never know whether I would have decided to be a man or a mouse, because just as quickly as the situation arose, so it was resolved. Instead of walking off with the camera, the one who'd picked it up said something to his companion, who promptly dropped his shorts. Focusing carefully, the camera-holder took a full-frontal close-up, wound the film on, then replaced the camera in the bag, and the pair of them strolled off down the beach. Childish? Maybe, but more amusing than theft.

Things seem to happen to me down by the seaside – perhaps that's why I don't shoot that many beach pictures. Last year, on a trip to the Caribbean, I was persuaded to go deep-sea fishing by a boat skipper I met on the beach. There I was, strapped into my swivel chair with a heavy-duty rod and dreaming of a 500lb marlin, when I noticed the horizon was doing strange things. On further inspection, I discovered that the shackle pin holding my chair to the deck had sheared. If I had caught that marlin, the rod, the chair and I would have been yanked overboard in a flash – I've no idea how long it takes to unstrap yourself from one of those chairs as you plummet towards the bottom of the ocean, but I do know that I don't want to find out.

So, more trips. In the new year I'll go on my usual travel-brochure binge, scooping up dozens and then spending a few evenings kidding myself it's all in the cause of work, but having a few daydreams along the way. Last year I seriously flirted with the idea of putting together a trip that would be profitable enough to enable me to hire Richard Branson's island. It was impossible, of course, but I had some harmless fun thinking about it.

****

DECEMBER

When I first started out as a photographer I was wedded to soft focus. Not only was it a style I found rewarding, but at that time it was also a very saleable technique. Fashions then changed, and the emphasis switched more and more to brightly-lit, pin-sharp pictures.

I have to take account of the laws of the marketplace, so I adapted my commercial style accordingly. But when shooting for my own pleasure, I've continued to produce quite a lot of soft-focus, grainy pictures, and still keep examples in my portfolio. They've rarely got me any work, I have to say – when Denise was my agent, she was forever coming back having taken my portfolio to one ad agency or another and saying how much the people she'd seen raved over my 'fuzzy stuff'. Quite often, the agency concerned would give me a job, but almost always it turned out that they wanted another brightly-lit, bang-in-focus number.

However, I sense a change in mood again, so I've started gently testing the soft-focus waters once more. Over the years I've experimented quite a lot with the technique; I've played around with a number of filters of varying degrees of strength, and for the strongest – in other words, softest – effect of all, I've used a stocking or a silk scarf over the lens.

For my last shoot before I flopped out for Christmas, I opted for a fairly minimal amount of soft-focus, using a filter called a Duto. The model, Laura, was a girl I'd photographed before, for calendars, and I chose her because I felt her looks would suit the romantic edge that soft-focus gives any subject. I also selected the location, a house in London that was recommended to me by another photographer, to chime in with the gentle mood I was aiming for. The resultant set proved very popular, so my instincts about a change of mood look like they're correct.

143

THE FINAL WORD

The last day of the year. Birthday and party time again. Looking back, I certainly feel more settled than I was 12 months ago. At the beginning of the year, my uncertainties about what to do with my old studio, and where to go if I left it, were colouring my attitude to my work and my clients – in short, I was not a happy chappie. Resolving that problem invigorated me, and my subsequent working relationship with Ralph has been a bonus that has benefited both of us.

As for the type of work I'm currently doing, I think I'd like to change the emphasis somewhat in the year to come. While I intend to keep up a certain quota of men's magazine work, and continue the profitable relationships with Moments and Dave Muscroft, I think I can now afford the luxury of doing more fashion and editorial work. Although often it isn't particularly well paid, I enjoy the varied creative challenges it offers.

Other ambitions include getting my golf handicap down to less embarrassing proportions, finding a permanent cure for the backache that afflicts me after a hard day's shooting, and never waking up with a hangover again. I don't seriously believe I'll achieve all, if any, of these – but, in my business, you have to be an optimist.

S P E C I F I C A T I O N S

Page IFC
Nikon F3   135mm lens
Fuji RDP 100   f11   250th
Speculative illustration
Kos Greece

Page 8
Nikon F3   105mm lens
Fuji RDP 100   f8   125th
Model folio
Denia Spain

Page 12
Nikon F3   85mm lens
Fuji RFP 50   f11.5   15th
Knave Magazine
Chiswick London

Page 21
Mamiya RB6/7   127mm lens
Kodak EPR 64   f11   30th
Moments Calendars
Sunningdale Berks

Page 26
Mamiya RB6/7   90mm lens
Fuji RDP 100   f8.5   15th
Moments Calendars
Hammerwood Park

Page 28-29
Nikon F2   105mm lens
Fuji 400D   f16   60th
Experimental
Studio London W1

Page 36-37
Mamiya RB6/7   127mm lens
Fuji RDP 100   f11.5   60th
Praline Germany
Gunthorpe Hall

Page 38
Nikon F3   85mm lens
Fuji RFP 50   f11   60th
Knave Magazine
Gunthorpe Hall

Page 42
Mamiya RB6/7   180mm lens
Kodak EPR 64   f11.5   125th
Model test
Studio London W1

Page 44-45
Mamiya RB6/7 180mm lens
Fuji RDP 100 f8.5 125th
Library illustration
Studio London W1

Page 46
Nikon F3 105mm lens
Fuji RFP 50 f11 8th
Knave Magazine
Canterbury Kent

Page 54
Mamiya RB6/7 180mm lens
Kodak EPR 64 f8.5 15th
Moments Calendars
East Sussex

Page 55
Mamiya RB6/7 180mm lens
Kodak EPR 64 f8.5 125th
Moments Calendars
Chiswick London

Page 57
Mamiya RB6/7 180mm lens
Kodak EPR 64 f11 15th
Moments Calendars
Ballroom SW4

Page 61
Mamiya RB6/7 127mm lens
Fuji RDP 100 f11 250th
Moments Calendars
Cranbourne Dorset

Page 62
Mamiya RB6/7 180mm lens
Kodak EPR 64 f8.5 125th
Moments Calendars
High Canons Herts

Page 66
Mamiya RB6/7 127mm lens
Fuji RDP 100 f11 15th
Moments Calendars
Greenwich

Page 70
Nikon F3 85mm lens
Fuji RFP 50 f11 125th
Stock Calendar
Kos Greece

Page 75
Nikon F3 135mm lens
Fuji RFP 50 f11 125th
Library
Kos Greece

Page 79
Nikon F3 200mm lens
Fuji RFP 50 f8 125th
Library
Kos Greece

Page 86-87
Mamiya RB6/7 250mm lens
Fuji RDP 100 f11 125th
Moments Visions
Tuscany Italy

Page 90
Mamiya RB6/7 180mm lens
Fuji RDP 100 f8 125th
Moments Visions
Tuscany Italy

Page 93
Mamiya RB6/7 127mm lens
Fuji RDP 100 f11 125th
Moments Visions
Tuscany Italy

Page 95
Mamiya RB6/7 180mm lens
Fuji RDP 100 f11 15th
Moments Calendars
Studio London W1

Page 99
Mamiya RB6/7 180mm lens
Fuji RDP 100 f11 125th
Moments Reflections
Studio London W12

Page 103
Mamiya RB6/7 250mm lens
Kodak EPR 64 f8 60th
Stock library
East Sussex

Page 106-7
Nikon F3 105mm lens
Fuji RFP 50 f11 125th
Oui USA
Tarifa Spain

Page 112
Nikon F3 85mm lens
Fuji RFP 50 f8 125th
Gallery USA
Algarve Portugal

Page 120
Nikon F3 105mm lens
Fuji RFP 50 f8.5 60th
Club International
Ealing London

Page 127
Nikon F3 85mm lens
Fuji RFP 50 f8 15th
Leyktur Sweden
Chiswick London

Page 130-1
Nikon F3 85mm lens
Fuji RFP 50 f11 60th
Knave Magazine
Los Angeles USA

Page 135
Nikon F3 50mm lens
Fuji RFP 50 f8 60th
Beihler Germany
Los Angeles USA

Page 139
Nikon F3 105mm lens
Fuji RFP 50 f11 60th
High Society USA
Studio London W12

Page 143
Nikon F3 105mm lens
Fuji RFP 50 f8.5 15th
Men Only
Sheen London

Page 144-5
Nikon F3 135mm lens
Fuji RFP 50 f8 250th
Stock library
Kos Greece

Page 152
Mamiya RB6/7 180mm lens
Kodak EPR 64 f11 125th
Kayser Hosiery
Studio London W1